A BOOK THAT WAS REJECTED

Written by
Professor Mirza Khalil Ahmad Beg

Translated by

Dr. Mohmad Ashraf Bhat
&
Dr. Mehnaz Rashid

FOREWORD

This book is the translation of my book, *Ek Bhasha Jo Mustarad Kar Di Gai* [A Book That Was Rejected] published in Urdu in 2007. The main purpose of writing this book was to reject the biased and prejudiced viewpoints of Gyan Chand Jain (1923- 2007), a prominent professor of Urdu and author of several high standard research works in Urdu. Lastly, in 2005 he published a book titled *Ek Bhasha: Do Likhawat, Do Adab* [*One Language: Two Scripts, Two Literatures*] which very much offended the entire Urdu speaking community. Most of them reacted very strongly to the views expressed by Prof. Jain in this book.

I am very grateful to my worthy student Dr. M. Ashraf Bhat and Dr. Mehnaz Rashid who did the translation work. Dr. Ashraf Bhat undertook the task of the publication of this book. I owe special thanks to him.

Mirza Khalil Ahmad Beg
Eldeco Elegance,
LUCKNOW
December 24, 2024

2

Copyright and all communications:
Interpreting & Translation Linguists Collective Agency
Website: https://bookpublishing.linguistscollective.info
Email: bp@linguistscollective.info
Phone: +44 (0)333 240 0139

ISBN: 978-1-916712-04-1

Originally published in Urdu in January 2007.
English translation published in March 2025.

PREFACE

At the outset it is essential to note that professor Beg's book, *Ek Bhasha Jo Mustarad Kar Di Gai* (A Book That was Rejected), is a collection of articles he authored in response to Professor Gyan Chand Jain's controversial work, *Ek Bhasha: Do Likhawat, Do Adab* (*One Language: Two Scripts, Two Literatures*). These articles by Professor Beg were originally published in *The Qaumi Aawaz*, New Delhi. The book, published in 2007 by the Educational Publishing House in Delhi, is divided into nine chapters. Professor Beg, a prominent Urdu linguist and the author of over twenty books, served as the Chairman and Professor of the Department of Linguistics at Aligarh Muslim University (AMU), one of India's oldest and premier universities, located in Aligarh, India. On the other hand, Professor Jain, a retired Urdu professor from the Central University of Hyderabad, was a distinguished Urdu critic, a specialist in Ghalib studies, and a renowned Urdu linguist. In recognition of his contributions to Urdu literature, Professor Jain was awarded the *Sahitya Akademi* Award for Urdu in 1982 and was honored with the *Padma Shri*, India's fourth-highest civilian award, in 2002.

On September 14, 2022, which is observed as *Hindi Diwas*, Adrija Roy Chowdhury authored an article titled "Hindi Diwas and the Historical Debate on Hindi's Status" for *The Indian Express*. In the article, he highlighted concerns about the contentious nature of Hindi's role in India. Roy noted, "Given that Hindi was the language spoken in many parts of North India, it was considered a suitable option for fostering national linguistic unity. However, this idea did not resonate well with the non-Hindi-speaking regions of the country." *Hindi Diwas* is an annual occasion that marks September 14, 1949, the day when the Constituent Assembly of India decided to adopt Hindi as the official language of the Union government, while granting English the status of an associate language for 15 years. The celebration of Hindi Diwas on September 14 was initiated by Prime Minister Pandit Jawaharlal Nehru.

The debate over the prominence of Hindi is longstanding. Roy Chowdhury further underscores the historical conflict between Urdu and Hindi, noting, "From the mid-1800s onwards, Urdu came into conflict with Hindi in what is now known as the 'Hindi belt.' Many believe that the seeds of the Hindu-Muslim conflict, which eventually led to the Partition of the subcontinent, were planted during the 19th-century Hindi-Urdu debate."

In this context, the relevance of the current review becomes even more pronounced, as it focuses on two primary perspectives. First, it addresses the ongoing debates surrounding Hindi's status as the official language of India. Second, it delves into the viewpoints of two prominent Urdu linguistic scholars in India, emphasizing their contributions to the extended and contentious Hindi-Urdu debates.

In the preface of Professor Beg's book, *Ek Bhasha Jo Mustarad Kar Di Gai* (A Book That was Rejected), it is evident that he was deeply disappointed with Professor Jain's controversial views on Urdu and Muslims. Professor Beg expresses his regret that Professor Jain's book, *Ek Bhasha: Do Likhawat, Do Adab* (*One Language: Two Scripts, Two Literatures*), does not seem to reflect the perspective of a dedicated Urdu enthusiast like Professor Jain but rather appears to be shaped by a conservative and biased viewpoint. Professor Beg presents several critiques of Professor Jain's work:

1. Professor Jain fails to provide a historical perspective on the Urdu-Hindi debate, offering excessive praise for Hindi while disparaging Urdu.

2. Professor Jain denies the historical precedence of Urdu, instead favoring the narrative of Hindi's primacy.

3. Professor Jain disregards the fact that Hindi was developed at Fort William College by Lallu Ji Lal, influenced by Englishmen, aligning with the 19th-century anti-Urdu movement and the aggressive promotion of Hindi.

4. Professor Jain shows a lack of respect for Urdu enthusiasts, expressing hostility towards the Urdu language and its literature, and associates them with religious animosity.

Professor Beg enumerates at least fifteen books that were written or translated into Urdu in northern India prior to the nineteenth century. He emphasizes that Urdu poetry began with Amir Khusro (1325-1353), with evidence of both poetry and prose present in the Deccan as early as the fourteenth century. By the eighteenth century, a substantial collection of Urdu literature existed in both northern and southern India. In contrast, there is a notable scarcity of Khari Boli Hindi literature from that period, with the few available samples either derived from Braj Bhasha or lacking authenticity. It is particularly surprising that Urdu authors have been incorrectly categorized as Hindi writers, as shown by Professor Jain's casual inclusion of Isvi Khan Bahadur's Urdu story, *Qissa Mehar Afroz-o-Dilber*, among Hindi writers. How can Isvi Khan Bahadur be considered a Hindi writer when his story is written in Urdu? (*One Language...*, p. 149).

While it is true that Urdu and Hindi share similarities at a fundamental level, as acknowledged by linguists, they are distinct languages in terms of their literary, scientific, cultural, and functional aspects. Although they may overlap significantly at a basic level, their differences become more evident upon closer analysis, setting them apart as separate languages. This distinction was likely recognized by the framers of the Indian Constitution, as both Hindi and Urdu are mentioned separately in the Eighth Schedule. However, Professor Jain dismisses this fact, referring to it as merely a "political strategy."

Despite significant similarities, notable differences emerge between the two languages in pronunciation, proverbs, idiomatic expressions, morphology (such as gender and number), particles, and other syntactic structures. They also differ in their literary traditions, devices, poetic forms, rhyme schemes, literary trends, and historical, cultural, and linguistic nuances. Additionally, the scientific, literary, and cultural terminology of both languages derives from different sources, and they are written in distinct scripts. Therefore, from a literary and cultural perspective, these languages cannot be considered identical, even if they may appear similar from a purely linguistic viewpoint.

While they share a common origin and exhibit structural and descriptive similarities, Urdu and Hindi have diverged significantly in their social, cultural, historical, and literary evolution, making them distinct from a sociolinguistic standpoint. Their differences in literary traditions, specialized vocabularies, and scripts further distinguish them. Beyond their similar grammatical structures, Urdu and Hindi differ in pronunciation, daily idiomatic expressions, proverbs, sayings, compound words, prefixes, suffixes, and markers for number and gender. Consequently, it is inaccurate to regard them as a single language. Moreover, Professor Jain's reference to King Koyi's *Chand Chhand Barnan ki Mehma* as the "first prose book of Khari Boli Hindi" on page 129 of *One Language...* is misguided. He appears unaware that the Hindi community discredited the authenticity of this book over fifty years ago.

ACKNOWLEDGEMENTS

We are deeply grateful to Professor M. K. A. Beg for granting us the opportunity to translate his book. Not only did he provide the manuscript for translation, but he meticulously reviewed every word of the translated text. Even during times when he was unwell, he responded to our texts, emails, and messages promptly and supported us wholeheartedly until the project was completed. His invaluable insights, guidance, and unwavering encouragement were instrumental in this endeavor.

Professor Beg is a distinguished academic and an exceptional scholar. He taught me during my postgraduate studies at Aligarh Muslim University (AMU) and has always been a source of inspiration. A dedicated linguist, he served as a Professor and Head of the Department of Linguistics at AMU, where he left an indelible mark. His scholarly contributions in Urdu linguistics have earned him global recognition. Seven Ph.D. dissertations have been written on his contributions. He has authored more than 20 books, significantly enriching the fields of Urdu linguistics, postmodern theory, and stylistics.

One memory that stands out vividly is from 2002, when Professor Beg asked me to accompany him to the editor's office where the department's journal was published. It was my paper that was to be edited. On our way, it started to rain, and we were drenched. Looking at me, he remarked, "This is how work is done." This simple yet profound moment encapsulated his sincerity and dedication to his work.

We also extend our heartfelt appreciation to our colleagues, and friends, who offered their support throughout this translation project. Their encouragement and belief in the importance of this work kept us motivated. Additionally, we acknowledge the valuable efforts of the editorial and publishing teams, whose meticulous attention to detail ensured the successful completion of this book. Above all, we dedicate this work to the scholars, students, and readers who continue to engage with the Urdu language and its rich literary heritage, ensuring its vitality and legacy for future generations.

Dr. Mohmad Ashraf Bhat
Jazan University, KSA

OVERVIEW

A Book That Was Rejected (*Ek Bhasha Jo Mustarad Kar Di Gai*) by Professor Mirza Khalil Ahmad Beg, translated by Dr. Mohmad Ashraf Bhat and Dr. Mehnaz Rashid, presents a critical rebuttal to Professor Gyan Chand Jain's *Ek Bhasha: Do Likhawat, Do Adab* (One Language: Two Scripts, Two Literatures). Originally published in Urdu in 2007, this book systematically deconstructs Jain's controversial claims regarding the historical and literary relationship between Urdu and Hindi. Comprising nine chapters, it highlights Jain's perceived biases, which, according to Beg, undermine the integrity of Urdu while unjustifiably elevating Hindi. Professor Beg contends that Jain's assertions, including the alleged inferiority of Urdu and its supposed resistance to Hindi, are academically flawed and driven by sectarian biases. He critiques Jain's failure to acknowledge Urdu's historical precedence over Hindi and its rich literary tradition dating back centuries. By omitting significant Urdu literary works and historical evidence, Jain's work, as Beg argues, distorts linguistic history to serve ideological ends. The book further examines the sociolinguistic evolution of both languages, demonstrating that while interconnected, they maintain distinct literary and cultural identities. Beg challenges the notion that Hindi organically developed, instead asserting that it was artificially constructed at Fort William College in the early 19th century. Beyond linguistic analysis, the book addresses the broader communal narratives that, according to Beg, seek to diminish Urdu's role in Indian heritage. *A Book That Was Rejected* is an essential scholarly response to linguistic imperialism, advocating for a more nuanced and historically grounded understanding of India's linguistic and cultural legacy.

TABLE OF CONTENTS

I.   **Foreword**   2

II. **Preface**   4

III. **Acknowledgement**   10

IV. **Overview**   12

Chapters

1. One Language: Two Scripts Two Literatures   15

2. Communal Thinking and Negative Perception   20

3. Urdu Language,
   Urdu Speaking Muslims and Urdu Literature   30

4. Khari Boil Hindi   42

5. Urdu's Precedence over Hindi   52

6. Hindi Imperialism and Urdu Language   62

7. The Outcome of *Prem Sagar*   79

8. Urdu, Hindi, Hindustani and The Fort William College   92

9. Anti-Urdu Movements and Tendencies   120

Notes   **146**

CHAPTER ONE

One Language: Two Scripts, Two Literatures

Professor Gyan Chand Jain's book, *One Language: Two Scripts, Two Literatures* (Delhi: Educational Publishing House, 2005), has sparked intense debate within academic circles. Many scholars who have read the book express deep disappointment, with some even voicing extreme frustration. Numerous recent articles have strongly criticized the book. Indeed, by publishing this work, Professor Jain has, in many eyes, irreparably damaged his reputation.

Professor Jain is a prominent Urdu scholar, esteemed researcher, and acclaimed author. He has been associated with Urdu language and literature for decades and has led the Urdu departments at various prestigious universities across India. Throughout his career, he devoted himself to advancing Urdu literature and language. However, in his later years, he developed Parkinson's disease, and by writing *One Language: Two Scripts, Two Literatures*, he stirred up significant controversy within the Urdu community.

On September 27, 2004, Professor Jain informed me that his book *One Language: Two Scripts, Two Literatures* would be published by a specific publisher and would be available in October. In that same letter, he shared, "I have a condition called Multiple System Atrophy. Science has little credible information about this disease, and there is no cure other than death." It is noteworthy that he managed to write such a book despite suffering from a serious illness and living in an area lacking a substantial body of Urdu-Hindi literature. To me, this book reflects his shared negative attitude towards the Urdu language, and I felt it necessary to address that. After reading the book, it becomes evident that Professor Jain holds a prejudiced stance against Urdu. He wrote this book from a one-sided, Hindu ideological perspective, as he himself acknowledges in the introductory remarks. Since the book was crafted with the intent of presenting the views of a specific religious community (Hinduism), it cannot be considered an impartial work.

Although the subject matter is fundamentally linguistic and academic, I believe that Professor Jain's portrayal of the Urdu-Hindi dialogue is excessively emotional and unpleasant. Consequently, the book is filled with irrelevant discussions, illogical arguments, and superfluous references. Moreover, it predominantly reflects the perspectives of Hindu writers who are narrow-minded, highly antagonistic, and biased against Urdu. Professor Jain considers the views of Muslim writers only when they align with his own ideology. He frames a linguistic issue through a sectarian lens, dividing it into Hindi and Urdu speakers. As a non-Muslim, he has distanced himself from Urdu speakers and aligned with Hindi speakers, advocating their viewpoints and ideology. It was our mistake to have regarded him as 'one of our own.'

It is regrettable that someone who dedicated his life to promoting Urdu language and literature, making significant contributions to its research and history, and earning high respect within Urdu literary circles, has turned against the language. He has aligned himself with critics of Urdu and disregarded his past contributions to the language. It is a profound loss for the Urdu language and its supporters when someone who once championed its cause becomes an adversary.

Reading this book reveals various facets of Professor Jain, who surprisingly defends Hindi while exhibiting hostility towards Urdu literature, which he characterizes as conservative and divisive. He even critiques the orthography of Urdu. Furthermore, he portrays Urdu as inferior to Modern Hindi and goes to great lengths to assert Hindi's superiority over Urdu. He also displays animosity towards

Muslims who speak Hindi, adopting a biased and communal attitude similar to that of other groups that hold anti-Muslim sentiments.

It is truly surprising to witness someone who spent his entire life deeply involved in Urdu, gaining respect, recognition, and prosperity through it, express such negative and unfounded views about the language. Despite listing Urdu as his mother tongue in census data, it is perplexing that he would adopt such a hostile position towards a language that has played such a significant role in his life.

Like many other Urdu scholars, I have greatly benefited from Professor Jain's wisdom, intellect, and scholarly contributions. I have always held him in high esteem as a distinguished Urdu scholar and respected his academic achievements. Moreover, I have admired and closely studied his linguistic works. However, after reading this particular book, my perception of his dedication to Urdu has diminished, as it appears that he has distanced himself from both the language and its scholars. Although Professor Jain claims, "I am still the admirer of Urdu as I used to be" (p. 11), it is difficult to accept this after reading the content of his book. Additionally, his statement, "I love Urdu more than Hindi" (p. 282), seems unconvincing. The reality is that this book has caused considerable distress among Urdu speakers and enthusiasts worldwide, profoundly affecting their sentiments towards the language.

CHAPTER TWO

Communal Thinking and Negative Perception

The title of the book *Ek Bhasha: Do Likhawat, Do Adab* (*One Language: Two Scripts, Two Literatures*) raises questions from the outset. The opening phrase is "Ek Bhasha..." yet the book is written in Urdu (using the Perso-Arabic script), not in Hindi. It is puzzling why, despite writing in Urdu, the author could not find an Urdu word for "language." Why did the author feel the need to use a Hindi term for "language"? Could it be that, after extensive engagement with Hindi, he could not identify a suitable equivalent in the Urdu lexicon? Why does the preference for Hindi terminology extend even to the title? From the very start, it is evident that Professor Jain has intentionally avoided using the Urdu term *"Zubaan"* for "language" and instead selected "Bhasha," a Hindi word. This choice struck me as unusual. How could someone who claims to be deeply familiar with Urdu literature and language use "Bhasha" instead of the more appropriate *"Zubaan"*? Could this be an early indication of a bias towards Hindi over Urdu? Then there is the issue of *"Do Likhawat"* (*Two Scripts*), a term that is both non-literary and inappropriate for the context. The proper term for "script" in Urdu is "Rasm-e-Khat." Why would a reputed scholar of Urdu, such as Professor Jain, choose to avoid using the correct term? The natural process of linguistic development in Urdu calls for the use of well-established terms like *"Zubaan"* for "language" and *"Rasm-e-Khat"* for "script," rather than adopting inaccurate alternatives like *"Bhasha"* and *"Likhawat."*

In the introduction, Professor Jain references two scholars, one of whom is the renowned Hindi scholar, the late Amrit Rai, who has been referred to as the 'Enemy of Hindi.' While this might sound disparaging, Rai was a highly respected scholar. The label may have been used ironically, given his critical stance on certain issues related to Hindi, but his contributions to Hindi literature were significant. However, the inclusion of such labels in the introduction raises doubts about the objectivity and academic integrity of the book. Additionally, there is no explanation for why so many individuals appear on Professor Jain's list of 'Enemies of Hindi.'

The book is organized into fourteen chapters, beginning with a preface and concluding with the last words, a conclusion, and an appendix. Professor Mohammad Hassan has contributed the foreword, providing a brief introduction to the book and emphasizing the importance of Hindustani alongside Hindi and Urdu. An introduction by Dr. Kamal Ahmad Siddiqui is also included. While the title *One Language: Two Scripts* is borrowed from Christopher R. King's work, Professor Jain's book diverges entirely in theme and content. Unlike Jain's book, King's work does not criticize Urdu or Muslims, nor does it display a preferential stance towards Hindi.

The first chapter, titled "Introduction" (pp. 13-43), is not only lengthy but also controversial and lacking in intellectual depth. Although Professor Jain claims to be writing from a position of truthfulness and asserts that "intellectuals' loyalty lies in the truth" (p. 13), upon reading these 31 pages, it becomes clear that they lack academic rigor and intellectual discourse. Instead, they appear to be a personal attack on Urdu, filled with biases that the author seems to have held for a long time.

The history of Urdu is misrepresented in this book. Muslim Urdu speakers, readers, and writers, as well as Urdu literary associations and organizations, are mocked and blamed. Even Urdu speakers from outside India, such as those in the United States and other countries, are accused of sectarianism and pessimism. This book does not come across as the work of a distinguished Urdu scholar like Professor

Jain but rather as that of someone with a conservative, prejudiced, and divisive mindset.

It is crucial to highlight some key points, particularly for Muslim Urdu scholars:

1. According to Professor Jain, Sir Syed Ahmad Khan became concerned when Hindus sought to replace Urdu with Hindi, which led him to criticize Hindus throughout the rest of his life (p. 18).

2. He referred to Sir Muhammad Iqbal as an enemy of Hindus and a "Hindu-hater." He also stated, "In his prose, wherever Iqbal mentions Hindus, he portrays them in an inferior position, although not so much in his poetry" (p. 21).

3. Molvi Abdul Haq, a significant figure in the Urdu Movement, was also criticized. It is mentioned that "the sole objective of the Urdu Movement was to divide the country and create Pakistan, which Molvi Abdul Haq wholeheartedly supported" (p. 39).

4. Malik Ram has been labeled as "a coward" for his inaction due to fear for his family, even though he is said to have been an Ahmadi Muslim at heart (p. 27).

5. Professor Jain accused Jagan Nath Azad of being a "Pakistani agent" due to his involvement in Iqbal

studies, stating, "Among all orientalists, Azad has been associated with Iqbal studies. It seems that Pakistan sent him to India as its representative" (p. 8).

6. Osmania University in Hyderabad has been characterized as "the Islamic Urdu university" and is seen as a significant outcome of the Urdu Movement (pp. 9-20).

7. The *Anjuman-e-Taraqqi-e-Urdu* (India) has been accused of aligning with the Muslim League since its inception (p. 39).

8. Professor Jain criticized the language of renowned Urdu writers like Mir Taqi Mir, Daag Dehlavi, and Mohammad Hussain, claiming that they exhibited "linguistic immaturity." He also mocked Malik Ram's accent and conversational style. Additionally, he claimed proficiency in all areas except Urdu, stating, "I am a master of all trades, but I don't know Urdu." (Note: In the book, a verse is misrepresented where the word "ek" was used instead of *"aik"* (p. 32).)

9. Regarding the term *Mehboob* (beloved), Professor Jain made serious allegations about several poets, stating that "many poets of Urdu, such as Momin,

Daag, Jigar, and Asghar, were associated with prostitutes (*tawaif*)" (p. 38).

10. Concerning Muslims, he wrote: "The policy of Muslims has been to impose their language and script upon the languages and scripts of the regions they conquered" (pp. 15-16).

11. Urdu-speaking Indian Muslims have been held responsible for the "Partition of India" (p. 5).

12. Pakistani Urdu speakers residing in the United States have been criticized for identifying themselves as Pakistanis rather than Americans. "It has been noted that almost all those who hold the US citizenship call themselves Pakistanis and not Americans. If there is an Urdu seminar, it is mentioned that it is organized by Pakistanis. Numerous weekly and monthly Urdu publications are issued in America and Canada, but Pakistani publications in English are more popular than Urdu ones. These publications are more inclined towards Pakistan. In such publications, Indians and Hindus are openly criticized, while Pakistanis are praised" (p. 23). Professor Jain concludes that "if Urdu speakers in other countries favor Pakistan, it is possible that Indian Muslims share similar views but

refrain from expressing them due to fear of the Hindu majority" (pp. 23-24).

13. Professor Jain also expressed his discontent with Pakistani Urdu speakers living in Pakistan. He criticized their school curriculum, stating, "It seems as if this curriculum was drafted by the Taliban of Afghanistan" (p. 24).

14. Driven by Hindi chauvinism, Gyan Chand Jain remarked: "It is not important that because we were raised through Urdu literature, we should consider Urdu literature as superior or older than Hindi literature" (p. 14).

15. Gyan Chand Jain firmly denies that Urdu is a language that unites Hindus and Muslims. He rejects the idea that Urdu emerged from mutual cooperation and interaction, stating that this is not a linguistic perspective but rather a sectarian perspective. He questions, "Why should Hindus show respect to the conquerors of the Somnath Temple, those who collected taxes from them, and those who destroyed Hindu culture?" (p. 147). Professor Jain frequently emphasizes that Urdu is not a symbol of unity and insists that the question of whether Urdu is a unifying

force or a symbol of division from the Indian (Hindi) language should not be discussed (ibid.).

Professor Jain, influenced by his ideology and a pessimistic thinking, fails to acknowledge that Khari Boli is the true root and origin of Urdu, rather than Arabic, Persian, or Turkish. Even more troubling is his omission of the fact that Sanskrit and Prakrit (*Tatsam* and *Tadbhav*), which make up 80% of the Urdu vocabulary, are fundamental to the language's structure. He also disregards the reality that while countless sentences and verses can be created without using Arabic or Persian words or grammar, it is impossible to form even a single sentence or verse without utilizing Indo-Aryan words or grammar. Urdu, a modern Indo-Aryan and Indian language like Hindi, is nonetheless depicted by him as "a symbol of separation from the Indian language." This portrayal highlights Professor Jain's lack of linguistic understanding and his narrow perspective on Indo-Aryan linguistics. Why is Urdu characterized as a language of division, while Hindi is not, despite both tracing their origins to Khari Boli? On what basis does Professor Jain label Urdu as a symbol of separatism, when, in reality, it has blended so seamlessly with Khari Boli that it embodies its essence? All linguists agree that Urdu is not an isolated language but rather a refined form of Khari Boli. In essence, Khari Boli could be considered synonymous with Urdu. Regrettably, Professor Jain holds a contrary viewpoint.

Such hostility and anti-Muslim sentiment are clearly evident throughout his book. Even serious topics are often treated with a sarcastic and dismissive tone. For instance, when referring to the predominantly Muslim neighborhood of Chitli Qabar in Delhi, near Jama Masjid, he derisively calls Chitli Qabar the "grave of Urdu." He writes:

"Now that Punjabi is widely spoken throughout Delhi, if you're searching for the 'grave of URDU,' you should go to Chitli Qabar and speak to a rickshaw puller or scooter driver, emphasizing/ geminating the /b/ in *Qabar* to demonstrate your fluency in Urdu. If you do this in Chitli Qabar, he will instantly recognize you as an outsider (a 'foreign chicken')" (p. 36).

What kind of academic language is reflected in that statement? Similarly, another example of Professor Jain's crude, disparaging, and elitist tone appears when he writes:

"Where once floats travelled, rickshaws now dominate, and they are all so dirty that even if Alexander the Great were to sit there, he would look like the illegitimate child of a village prostitute" (p. 36).

CHAPTER THREE

Urdu Language, Urdu Speaking Muslims and Urdu Literature

In *"One language: Two Scripts, Two Literatures"*, Professor Jain has deviated from the main topic and vented his resentment toward the Muslims who speak the language even presently, and according to him have ruled the country for 600 years (p. 146). Professor Jain characterizes those Muslims as temple destroyers (specifically referring to the Somnath temples), tax exploiters, and as opponents of Hindu culture (p. 147).

Professor Jain has not voiced his concern regarding the brutal killings of Muslims during the demolition of the Babri mosque on December 6, 1992. He described the attacks on a few temples in the neighboring countries in retaliation for the Babri demolition as "revenge" and expressed his sorrow over them. He harshly criticized Jagan Nath Azad, one of India's sensitive and kind poets, for publishing a poem about the destruction of the Babri Masjid in which he expressed his sympathy and concern (p. 215). Additionally, Professor Jain expressed sympathy for the exiled Bangladeshi writer Taslima Nasreen, who was banned from her country, because she wrote the novel *Lajja* in protest of the destruction of temples in her nation (p. 215). What kind of philosophy does Professor Jain uphold when he accuses a renowned poet from his own country of betraying his nation simply for writing poems protesting the mosque's destruction, while supporting an unfamiliar foreign author because she wrote a book about the demolition of temples in Bangladesh?

There is no doubt that the Hindu fundamentalists responsible for the destruction of the Babri Masjid were also indirectly responsible for the damage to temples in neighboring countries. On this issue, Professor Jain has aligned himself with the leading fascist political party of India, asserting that the site was no longer a mosque, stating, "that has already been converted into a temple." His statement is:

"The Babri Masjid opened between 1985 and 1986. Hindus were allowed to perform rituals, and Muslims were not allowed to enter the premises. So, in 1992, the building that was demolished was either a mosque or had already been transformed into a temple?" (p. 215).

Why does Professor Jain continue to bring up such sensitive topics in a book that is supposed to be linguistic and academic?

It is essential to challenge the way Professor Jain has harshly blamed, accused, and held Urdu-speaking Muslims accountable. These allegations are baseless; they stem solely from his biased perspective. When someone is consumed by negative thoughts, they lose their ability to reason, exercise restraint, and remain impartial. This mindset can also lead to a sense of frustration, driving them to write whatever comes to mind without consideration for objectivity. Professor Jain's animosity towards Urdu and Muslims stems from his negative mindset and pessimistic thought process. In his book, Professor Jain states, "More unfortunate than favoritism is to give religious and communal orientation to the academic discourses" (p. 14). However, he himself is guilty of infusing a religious and communal bias into academic discourse, with this book serving as a prime example. It is deeply regrettable that Professor Jain has interpreted every subject—whether literature, history, politics, culture, language, or script—through a religious and communal lens. These discussions clearly reflect his biased perspective. He writes:

"The burden of the Two Nation Theory is always on the shoulders of Muslims in India. Common Hindus do not comprehend why Muslims should be treated equally to Hindus" (p. 33).

Professor Jain fails to recognize that no Muslim in India, whether they speak Urdu or another language, subscribes to the Two Nation Theory. His claims are based solely on false accusations and his biased thinking. He questions why Muslims should be treated equally to Hindus, but this viewpoint reveals his intellectual narrowness. The Indian Constitution guarantees equal rights to all citizens of India. According to these constitutional rights, all religious communities in India, including Muslims and Hindus, are entitled to equal treatment.

Professor Jain's communal and prejudiced attitude is further evident in his harsh language towards Indian Urdu-speaking Muslims, whom he blames for the creation of Pakistan. He references a statement from one of his female relatives, an immigrant to India after the partition, who remarked, "After looking at the Muslims of Delhi and UP, she stated that they wanted the partition of India; why are they here then?" (p. 25).

On the same page, he reiterates a similar view, suggesting that Muslims in India desired partition, which he believes left them feeling "psychologically weak and inferior." He claims that the "Muslim minority living in India are psychologically inferior and weak, regardless of whether their social or economic status is better or not. The only thing that can be said to them is: it's better to treat yourself" (p. 25).

If Professor Jain could set aside his anti-Muslim prejudice and communal mindset, he might consider how Muslims could be held accountable for India's partition. Are those Muslims who chose to remain in their beloved country, rather than migrating to Pakistan after the Partition, to blame? Are the generations of Muslims born after the partition responsible for this division of India? Why should Muslims who chose to stay in their homeland instead of moving to Pakistan be held accountable? And how can the subsequent generations of Muslims, born long after the Partition, be blamed for an event they did not experience?

After reading the cited statements from Professor Jain's book, it is not surprising that a work intended to be academic is filled with prejudice and communal biases.

Professor Jain's bigotry is also evident in how he categorizes secular Urdu writers into "Hindu Urdu writers" and "Muslim Urdu writers" based on their religion. He falsely accuses Muslim writers of disregarding Hindu writers. He states, "Even well-known Hindu writers must be cautious; if they want to assert themselves in the Urdu community, they need to appease Muslims" (p. 26).

Most would agree that, in recent history, among Hindus, figures like Firaq Gorakhpuri as a poet, Krishan Chander as a novelist, and Malik Ram as a researcher have made significant contributions to Urdu literature. Can Professor Jain name any Muslims who were praised or flattered by these Hindu writers as they achieved fame, respect, status, and awards? Can he also specify which Muslims are being praised by contemporary Hindu writers as they establish themselves in the Urdu literary community? Furthermore, did Professor Jain himself flatter or seek the approval of any Muslim scholars to gain the reputation, respect, and status he enjoyed within the Urdu community?

As mentioned in chapter one, Professor Jain has a negative view of Urdu literature, claiming that Hindus have been disrespected within it (p. 200). He has attempted to "reveal" examples from older Urdu stories where, in his view, prominent Hindu figures have not been given due respect. It would have been more balanced if he had also provided similar examples from Hindi literature where Muslims have been insulted, humiliated, and where their community and religious sentiments have been hurt.

In reality, there are numerous poems and verses in Urdu literature that celebrate and honor Hindu religious deities and leaders. For instance, Iqbal's poem "Ram" reflects his deep admiration for Ram Chandra Ji, referring to him as "Imam-e-Hind."

Indeed, countless poems and verses in Urdu literature pay tribute to Hindu religious leaders. In Iqbal's poem 'Ram,' for example, Iqbal expresses profound respect and gratitude for Ram Chandra Ji, calling him 'Imam-e-Hind.' Similarly, a Muslim poet, Amir Minai, did not hesitate to praise Goddess Kali (*Kali Maa*).

Professor Jain has also accused Urdu literature of promoting "gender violence" (see p. 189 for details). He presents examples from early Urdu literature where a Muslim man falls in love with a Hindu woman who then converts to Islam, abandoning her Hindu faith. He highlights instances where a (female) beloved embraces the religion of her (male) lover (Islam). According to Professor Jain, such acts represent not only "sexual violence" but also "religious violence." This perspective is clearly a product of Professor Jain's limited understanding, as historical records indicate that Hindu-Muslim marriages were once common during the Middle Ages. These unions were characterized by mutual consent, with no element of force or violence, marking a golden period of Hindu-Muslim social and cultural harmony.

Thus, such practices should not be viewed through a sectarian or religious lens. In fact, neither kings nor commoners found fault with these unions or opposed them. History records that Amir Khusro was born to a Hindu mother, and Jodha Bai was the wife of Emperor Akbar. The wife of Jehangir and other high-ranking officials' wives were also Hindu. Numerous examples exist of Hindu women marrying Muslim men or Muslim women marrying Hindu men out of mutual choice, with no connection to sexual or religious coercion—this remains true even today. So, what is the issue if these historical facts and cultural practices are reflected in literature, including books, stories, poems, and other works? To portray such consensual practices as communal is merely a reflection of frustration.

Does Professor Jain also dislikes the following literary discourses?

"In his Persian quatrains, Amir Khusrau tried to hit on and lure Hindu lovers and children. Mulla Sheree (?) has insultingly addressed/spoke harshly to the (*Qashqa Jabin*), [Hindu] women with saffron mark on their foreheads. Qazalbash Khan Umid and Faaiz troubled Baman's daughter and Khatrani... Even in religious works (Masnavi) 'The Spiritual Couplets' like Munir Shikoh Abadi's "*Meraj-ul-Mazameen*" it was not refrained from discussing Hindu women's beauty while describing spiritual themes.'" (pp. 192-193).

While writing this, Professor Jain seems to have forgotten that he was analyzing a literary work, not a divine text. Viewing everything through a sectarian lens, he arrives at the following conclusion:

"In (Masnavis) 'The Spiritual Couplets' and (*Dastans*) 'fables/literary anecdotes,' romance with non-Muslim women, religious conversion, and targeting Hindu women through poetry were all considered permissible under the Muslim rule" (p. 193).

Professor Jain has lamented and expressed his displeasure about Muslim men having affairs with Hindu women and the conversion of Hindu women to Islam in literary works. But the fact neglected to mention or not mentioned in the literary world, however, is that there has been a Muslim character in literature who fell in love with a Hindu woman and sacrificed everything for her, even adopting Hindu customs and culture. She also, wears the clothes of Brahmin, changes her name to a Hindu name, and wanders in the temples of Mathura in search of her beloved. This figure was none other than the famous writer Mohammad Afzal Afzal (1625) of Jahanghir's era, the author of the authentic poetic work "*Bikat Kahani*", who changed his name to "Gopal" after adopting Hindu way of life. His practice of Hindu religion was not imaginary, for he was so familiar with Hindu religion that he became a temple priest.

In *Gulistan-e-Saedi*, it is stated that "when it comes to love, the distinction between king and slave disappears." Similarly, in true love, the difference in religion between lover and beloved becomes irrelevant. Lovers transcend religious boundaries and embrace a shared faith—the faith of love.

Professor Masood Hussain Khan, who has reviewed *Bikat Kahani*, writes about Gopal:

> *"Gopal is the name Afzal adopted during his time in Mathura. In this act of beauty and love, it is fitting that Afzal would choose the name Gopal, as it is one of the names of Lord Krishna" (Bakat Kahani, p. 84).*

After extensive research, Professor Masood provides a compelling account of Gopal/Afzal:

"Teaching was his profession. From the start, he was deeply captivated by love, and in his later years, he became fully immersed in the Hindu way of life. He renounced Islam and adopted the qualities of Majnoon, embracing asceticism and spirituality. He donned the attire of a Brahmin, became a disciple of a temple priest, and devoted himself to studying Hinduism, mastering its various arts and disciplines. Impressed by his dedication, the Guru appointed him as his successor, and when the Guru eventually succumbed to illness, he declared that Afzal (Gopal) should be recognized as his successor." (Bikat Kahani, pp. 24-25).

Does Professor Jain still believe that, in matters of love and romance, it is only Hindu women who abandon their religion, while Muslim men remain steadfast in their faith? One of Mir Taqi Mir's verses suggests that he too may have been involved in a romantic relationship with a Hindu woman:

"Mir ke deen-o-mazhab ka, poochhte kya ho unhon ne to kashka khaincha, dair mein baitha, kab ka tark-e-Islam kiya"

"Why do you inquire about Mir's religion or creed? For he Sits in temples, a tilak on his forehead, having long forsaken Islam."

CHAPTER FOUR

Khari Boli Hindi

In his book, Professor Jain criticizes the Urdu community for their objections to the historical narrative of Hindi literature. According to him, the objection is as follows:

"Khari Boli Hindi is a new language that emerged at Fort William College during British rule. Its sole purpose was to provide a common language for the Hindus" (p. 118).

However, what Professor Jain sees as objectionable is actually a well-established fact. It is surprising that he blames the Urdu community for raising this issue. A closer linguistic examination of Hindi reveals that this perspective was first put forward by Hindi writers themselves, followed by scholars like Grierson and others.

Ayodhya Prasad Khatri was a prominent Hindi poet and intellectual of the second half of the 19th century. He was the strongest supporter of Hindi poetry in Khari Boli. In 1884, he published a book under the title *Khari Boli ki Shayari* (The Poetry of Khari Boli), which ignited a significant debate about the relationship between Khari Boli, Braj Bhasha, Hindi, and Urdu. He considered Braj Bhasha and Khari Boli as entirely separate languages but treated

Khari Boli and Urdu as a single language. He referred to Urdu poetry as the poetry of Khari Boli. Although he believed that the fundamental difference between Hindi and Urdu resides in their respective scripts, he also claimed that Urdu has an earlier historical development than Hindi, suggesting that Hindi is, in essence, derived from Urdu.

Ayodhya Prasad Khatri asserts that the "current, artificial Hindi" was developed from Urdu by deliberately removing Arabic and Persian words. He states: *"Modern Hindi was developed by intentionally eliminating Arabic and Persian elements from Urdu and replacing them with typical Sanskrit words" (p. 167).*

Professor Jain discusses Ayodhya Prasad Khatri and cites the five styles of Khari Boli, yet he omits any mention of Khatri's linguistic viewpoint, which goes against academic integrity. These five Khari Boli linguistic styles are equated with Hindi by Professor Jain, further contradicting scholarly standards (see p. 181).

Another Hindi writer, Chandra Dhar Sharma 'Glarie', holds a similar view regarding the origin of Hindi as Ayodhya Prasad Khatri. In his book *Purani Hindi* (Old Hindi), Glarie writes:

"The oldest poetry created by Hindus corresponds with Braj Bhasha or Purvi, Awadhi, Rajasthani, Gujarati, and 'Khari Boli'. From contemporary poetry and prose of Khari Boli or Pakki Boli or Rekhta or Present Hindi, it is evident that Hindi evolved from Urdu by replacing Arabic and Persian words with Sanskrit terms that have become either *Tatsama* or *Tadbhava*" (p. 107).

The renowned Hindi poet Jagan Nath Das Ratnakar similarly believes that Khari Boli Hindi is a refined version of Urdu, into which '*Bhakha*' words were initially incorporated, followed by Sanskrit terms over time. He explains: "The language currently known as Khari Boli is, in my view, actually a refined form of Urdu. It originally developed by integrating words from *Bhakha*, and gradually Sanskrit words were added" (*Khari Boli Ka Aandholan*, p. 21).

In this context, Khari Boli refers to Khari Boli Hindi, while *Bhakha* refers to Braj Bhasha. Historically, Hindus have been closely connected to Braj Bhasha from a religious standpoint, as it is the language of the region where Lord Krishna was worshiped. From a literary perspective, Braj Bhasha also held significant importance and was once the dominant language spoken in North India. For this reason, many Hindu writers consider Braj Bhasha to be the true form of Hindi spoken today and believe that modern Hindi has evolved from it. Although this belief is not accurate, it is undeniable that the early literary works of Braj Bhasha had a substantial influence on Khari Boli Hindi when it began to develop in the nineteenth century. This influence is evident in works like Lallu Ji Lal's *"Prem Sagar,"* published at Fort William College. Numerous Hindi scholars and academics have recognized Braj Bhasha's impact on *"Prem Sagar,"* including Jagan Nath Das Ratnakar. Based on this viewpoint, Ratnakar argued that since Urdu already existed and contained elements of Braj Bhasha and Sanskrit, it ultimately gave rise to Hindi, suggesting that Hindi originated from Urdu.

A notable aspect of Professor Jain's perspective is that he accuses the Urdu community of objecting to the history of Hindi by asserting that "New Khari Boli Hindi originated at Fort William College in 1800. Before that, Hindi didn't exist... Its first book is *'Prem Sagar'* by Lallu Lal, in whose prose Arabic and Persian words have been replaced by Sanskrit words" (p. 126). Professor Jain notes that G.A. Grierson was the first to highlight this fact, writing in the 1896 preface of Lallu Lal's *Lal Chandrika*: "Earlier, there was no sign of such a language in India. For this reason,

Lallu Lal wrote '*Prem Sagar*,' creating a new language" (*One Language...*, p. 126).

Professor Jain further lists R.W. Frazer, who in his *Literary History of India* (1915), writes: "Two Pandits, Lallu Lal and Sadal Mishar, should be considered the inventors of Modern Hindi" (ibid).

When Professor Jain attributes such "objections" about the history of Hindi to the Urdu community, he should have substantiated his claims with specific examples from within the Urdu community. However, he fails to provide such examples. As far as my knowledge extends, no one from the Urdu community in the 19th century objected to the history of Hindi in this manner. In fact, such an objection was first recorded by the Hindi scholar and intellectual Ayodhya Prasad Khatri. Nine years later, in 1896, Grierson echoed this objection, followed by Frazer in 1915. Later, in 1920, Frank E. Keay expressed a similar opinion in his book *A History of Hindi Literature*. This is not an "objection" but rather a fact that was initially noted by Ayodhya Prasad Khatri and subsequently supported by many English and Hindi authors. While Urdu scholars agreed with these Hindi writers, they have been accused of challenging the history of Hindi. Among the Urdu scholars mentioned by Professor

Jain in this context are Farmaan Fatehpuri, whose book *Hindi Urdu Tanaza* (*Hindi Urdu Conflict*) was published in 1993, and Shams-ul-Rehman Farooqi, whose book *Urdu Ka Ibtidayi Zamana* (*The Initial Era of Urdu*) was also released in 1993. Thus, when Urdu scholars repeated a fact that had been acknowledged over 100 years ago by English and Hindi scholars, they were accused of "countering or challenging" the history of Hindi (*Ek Basha...*, Chapter 8).

Let's examine Grierson's work to determine whether his views evolved over 25-30 years. Grierson first expressed his opinion on the creation of a new language, Hindi, in 1896 while writing the preface to Lallu Lal's book *Chandrika*. However, even after the publication of his renowned work *Linguistic Survey of India* in 1927, his opinion remained unchanged. He further elaborated that Lallu Ji's Hindi was derived from Urdu, with Indo-Aryan words replacing Persian ones. This observation by Grierson, recorded in Volume 9, Part I of his *Linguistic Survey of India*, states:

> "This Hindi, therefore, or, as it is sometimes called, 'High Hindi,' is the prose literary language of those Hindus of Upper India who do not employ Urdu. It

is of modern origin, having been introduced under English influence at the commencement of the last century. Up until then, when a Hindu wrote prose and did not use Urdu, he wrote in his own dialect— Awadhi, Bundeli, Braj Bhakha, or another. Lallu Lal, under the guidance of Dr. Gilchrist, changed all this by writing the well-known *Prem Sagar*, a work which, as far as the prose portions were concerned, was practically written in Urdu, with Indo-Aryan words substituted wherever a writer in that form of speech would use Persian ones" (p. 46).

Similarly, another English writer, Frank A. Keay, notes in his book *History of Hindi Literature*:

"Modern High Hindi was developed from Urdu by the exclusion of Persian and Arabic words and the substitution of those of pure Indian origin, Sanskrit or Hindi" (p. 46).

In the same book, Grierson further observes:

"Lallu Ji Lal was a Brahmin whose family originally hailed from Gujarat but had long been settled in North India. Under the guidance of Dr. John Gilchrist, he and Sadal Mishra became the architects of modern 'High Hindi.' While many dialects of Hindi were spoken in North India, the language of refined speech among those unfamiliar with Persian was Urdu. However, Urdu contained a significant vocabulary derived from Persian and Arabic, languages closely associated with Islam. There was a strong need for a literary language for Hindi-speaking people that would be more appealing to Hindus. This was achieved by taking Urdu, removing words of Persian or Arabic origin, and replacing them with words of Sanskrit or Hindi origin" (p. 83).

Regarding the new language of the Hindus, Keay writes:

"The Hindi of Lallu Ji Lal was really a new literary dialect. This 'High Hindi', or 'Standard Hindi' as it is also called, has had however a great success. It has been adopted as the literary speech of millions in North India. Poetical works still continue to be written in Braj Bhasha, or Awadhi, or other old dialects, as High Hindi has not been much used for poetry. But whereas before this time prose works in Hindi were very rare, from now onwards an extensive prose literature began to be produced." (Pp.83–84).

One of the notable Hindu writers and historians, Dr. Tara Chand, delivered an insightful radio talk titled "What is Hindustani?" discussing the creation of a new language at Fort William College, which is worth mentioning:

"Lallu Lal Ji, Badal Mishra, Bini Narayan, and others were appointed by the Fort William College authorities to develop prose literature for Hindus. They faced numerous challenges. While Braj Bhasha was the language of literature, it had no tradition of prose writing. Consequently, they had to adopt the language used by Meer Aman, Afsoos, and others, omitting Arabic and Persian words and replacing them with Sanskrit and Hindi terms. As a result, two languages, radically altered from their original forms, emerged within less than ten years under the influence of external forces. Despite their common ancestry, both languages bore similarities. They shared a similar structure and outlook, but their orientations differed. This seemingly minor divergence has placed the entire country at risk. Since then, we have been walking on two separate paths." (*Shamsul Rehman Farooqi, Initial Stage of Urdu*, pp. 49-50).

The assertion by the renowned Hindi author Ram Chandri Shakil in his book *Hindi Sahitya Ka Itihas* (*A History of*

Hindi Literature, p. 365) is particularly relevant here, as it supports what Lallu Ji Lal mentioned in *Prem Sagar*:

"Had Lallu Lal not been proficient in Urdu, he would not have been able to replace the Arabic and Persian words in *Prem Sagar*. Even those well-versed in Sanskrit found it difficult to distinguish and identify many Arabic and Persian terms from the everyday spoken language" (p. 185, Gyan Chand Jain's *Linguistic Study*, 1st Edition).

All these statements and claims regarding the creation of a new language at Fort William College—where Arabic and Persian words were removed to shape Hindi or Khari Boli Hindi—come from Hindi, Hindu, and English writers. Yet, Professor Jain attributes the responsibility for this to the Urdu speaking community.

CHAPTER FIVE

Urdu's Precedence over Hindi

In the introduction of his book, Professor Jain explicitly states that he does not believe Hindi originated from Urdu and clearly expresses his preference/favour for Hindi:

"It is not important that we grew up with the roots of Urdu literature, so it is not our duty to regard Urdu literature as dominant over Hindi" (p. 14).

Despite being an Urdu scholar who emerged from the Urdu literary tradition, he rejects this view. However, many scholars and intellectuals with a background in Hindi acknowledge Urdu's historical precedence over Hindi. Given Professor Jain's proficiency in Hindi, it is highly likely that he has read *Hindi Bhasha Ka Itihas* (*History of Hindi*) by Dhirendra Verma, a well-regarded expert in Hindi literature and linguistics. On page 60 of this work, Verma states: "From a historical perspective, Khari Boli Urdu predates Khari Boli Hindi in usage."

Does Professor Jain still deny that Urdu existed before Hindi? Notably, Dhirendra Verma views Urdu not as a sister language of Hindi, but as an independent language, stating:

"Modern literary Hindi and Urdu both originated from Khari Boli" (p. 56). He further explains, "From a grammatical standpoint, the two literary languages do not differ significantly; they share the same roots and origin. However, they diverge in terms of literary context, vocabulary, and script" (p. 60). According to Verma, Urdu has been present in Delhi since the time when Muslims established Delhi as their central hub. He elaborates:

"After entering India, Muslims established Delhi as their centre. Consequently, Muslims who spoke Turkish, Arabic, and Persian began to gradually learn the local language of Delhi by interacting with the inhabitants. It was natural for them to incorporate foreign words into the local language. The first use of this evolving language was noted in the royal military camps, and it eventually became known as Urdu— a language that developed through the integration of foreign elements into the local Delhi dialect. The word 'Urdu' means 'camp' or 'market' in Turkish."(ibid. p. 60)

Muslims first arrived in Delhi in the latter half of the twelfth century (1193 AD) and encountered the Khari Boli language. As Arabic, Persian, and Turkish words were absorbed into Khari Boli, the language evolved into Urdu. In this discussion, Dhirendra Verma does not mention Khari

Boli Hindi, which implies that Khari Boli Hindi did not exist in northern India when Muslims first arrived in Delhi, nor shortly thereafter. Despite this, Professor Jain maintains that Urdu existed before Hindi and dismisses the theory that Khari Boli Hindi existed as early as 1100 AD as mere conjecture.

Dhirendra Verma identifies Khari Boli as the root of Urdu, asserting that Khari Boli Urdu is older than Khari Boli Hindi. He refers to the earlier form of Urdu as "*Hindvi*" and describes it as a language that emerged in the Deccan in the fourteenth century. Simply put, he treats *Hindvi* as synonymous with Deccani Urdu, noting:

"*Hindvi* or Deccani Urdu originated in South India following Mohammad Tughluq's invasion in 1326 AD. The early poets of *Hindvi* were Sufi Muslims who composed their works to spread their religious teachings. This language was not written in Devanagari script but in an older form of Khari Boli" (p. 80).

It is important to highlight that Dhirendra Verma, a prolific Hindi author, does not regard "Decaani Urdu" as either Deccani Hindi (or Dheccani Hindi) or as a sister language of Hindi. He treats Hindi and Urdu as distinct and separate languages. Verma asserts that Literary Khari Boli developed into two distinct languages—Khari Boli Urdu and Khari Boli Hindi—with Khari Boli Urdu emerging first. This perspective, which Verma, a respected Hindi scholar and intellectual, maintains, supports the idea that Urdu literature predates Hindi literature. However, Urdu scholar Professor Jain rejects this fact, which is rather puzzling.

In addition to Dhirendra Verma, other Hindi scholars have also acknowledged Urdu's precedence over Hindi. They have explicitly pointed out the lack of a literary tradition in Khari Boli Hindi before the 19th century. Retired Professor Shati Kanth Mishra of Banaras Hindu University (BHU) writes in his book *Khari Boli ka Andholan* (*The Movement of Khari Boli*):

"It cannot be said that there was any literary tradition in Khari Boli (Hindi) before the 19th century in North India."

Here, 'Khari Boli' specifically refers to Khari Boli Hindi. However, at least 15 books were written or translated in Khari Boli Urdu in North India before the 19th century. These works include:

1. *Karbal Katha* (1732/33) by Fazl-i-Ali Fazli, Mali Ram, and Mukhtar Aldin Ahmad

2. *Qissa Mehar Afroz-o-Dilber* (1732-59) by Isvi Khan Bahadur and Masood Hussain Khan

3. *Sharh 'Ras Chandrika'* (1752) by Isvi Khan Bahadur

4. *Nov Tarz-Marsa* (1774-75) by Mir Mohammad Hussain Ata Khan Tehseen and Nur ul Hussain Hashmi

5. *Tafseer-i Muradiya* (1771-72) by Shah Muradullah Ansari

6. *Qissa Ahwali Roheela* (1774-81) by Rustom Ali Bijnori

7. *Tarjuma-yi Quran* (1787/88) by Shah Rafi ud Din

8. *Tarjuma-yi Quran* (1790/91) by Shah Abdul Qadir

9. *Tafseer-i Rafiee [Surah Baqarah]* (1790/91) by Shah Rafi ud Din

10. *Tafseer-ul Quran* (1791/92) by Shah Haqani

11. *Ajaaibul Qasas* (1792/93) by Shah Alam Thani and Rahat Afza Bukhari

12. *Qissa Mulk Mohammad wa Gageeti Afroz* (1793/94) by Mehar Chand Khatri Mehar

13. *Jazb-e-Ishq* (1797/98) by Shah Hussain Haqeeqat

14. *Nov Aayinee Hind* (1798/99) by Mehar Chand Khatri Mehar

15. *Silki Gehar* (1799/1800) by Insha Allah Khan Insha and Imtiaz Ali Khan Arshi.

All of these books were available in northern India before the 19th century. Urdu poetry was first initiated by Amir Khusro (1325-1353). After that, traces of poetry and prose can be found in the Deccan from the 14th century. In the 18th century, there was a substantial amount of Urdu literature available in both northern and southern India. However, there are no traces of Khari Boli Hindi literature from this era. The few samples that exist are either taken from Braj Bhasha or are not authentic. It is surprising that even Urdu authors were often classified as Hindi authors. For example, Professor Jain casually included the renowned North Indian prose writer Isvi Khan Bahadur's "*Qissa Mehar Afroz-o-Dilber*" among Hindi authors. Since this story is written in Urdu, how can Isvi Khan Bahadur be considered a Hindi writer? (*A Book...*, p. 149). It is ironic that in his book's discussion (pp. 302-306), Professor Jain listed Urdu literary works published before 1800 but did not include Isvi Khan Bahadur's *Qissa Mehar Afroz-o-Dilber*. One might ask why Professor Jain excluded this significant Urdu work, published between 1732 and 1759.

Hindi scholars like Shati Kanth Mishar have acknowledged that before the 19th century, there was no literary tradition in Khari Boli Hindi, nor was there prose or poetry in this language. This is because Khari Boli Hindi did not exist before 1800, making a literary tradition impossible without the language itself.

A renowned Hindi scholar, Chandar Dhar Sharma Gilarie, attributes the emergence of Khari Boli to the influence of Muslims, treating Khari Boli as Urdu and considering Hindi to have evolved from Urdu. In his book *Purani Hindi* (*Old Hindi*), he states:

"The genesis of Hindi prose writing begins with Lallu Lal Ji. The ancient Hindi prose and poetry in Khari Boli have been influenced by Muslim culture" (*Purani Hindi*, p. 108).

Vishwanath Prasad Mishra, another Hindi scholar with a deep interest in the linguistic relationship between Urdu and Hindi, initially focused on Rekhta. After extensive study, he concluded that Rekhta and Khari Boli are the same language, differing only in name. He argued that Rekhta is a style that emerged from Khari Boli with Arabic and Persian influences, which later evolved into Urdu, eventually giving rise to Hindi. According to Omkar Rahi:

Mishra also noted that to distinguish Urdu from local languages, Arabic and Persian terms were removed from Urdu, which was then named Hindi, Bakha, or Khari Boli Hindi.

Bhartendu Harishchandra, a prominent 19th-century Hindi scholar, also considered Khari Boli to be Urdu. In the preface of his book *Agarwalu ki Utpatti* (*Birth of the Aggarwals*), he wrote: "Aggarwals are from the northwest, and their language (of both men and women) is Khari Boli, which is Urdu."

Bhartendu's statement provides valuable insight, especially given Professor Jain's belief that Urdu was limited to the formal domain and used primarily by Hindi men, not women (*One Language*, p. 28). Bhartendu, like other 19th-century scholars, regarded Khari Boli and Urdu as the same language. This belief led many Hindu scholars to favor Braj Bhasha for Hindi poetry, as they felt that poetry written in Khari Boli would be considered Urdu.

According to Hindu writers and historical records, it is evident that Khari Boli Hindi emerged in the early 19th century. When Fort William College was established in Calcutta in 1800, it marked the beginning of this language.

Gilchrist instructed Lallu Ji Lal to use Urdu, which was already prevalent in northern India, as the foundation. He replaced Persian and Arabic words with Sanskrit terms and chose to write in the Devanagari script, creating a new language known as Khari Boli Hindi. Lallu Ji Lal wrote *Prem Sagar* (The Ocean of Love) in this newly constructed language in 1803. Another scholar at Fort William College, Sadal Mishra, wrote the story *Nasikhtiya Pakhiyaan* adopting the same language. Both of the texts were translated from Sanskrit, and the linguistic approach adopted in these works led to the emergence of a new language. Bhartendu Harishchandra referred to Lallu Ji Lal's Khari Boli Hindi as "*Nayi Bhasha*" (*New Language*) in his book *Hindi Bhasha*. Thus, Urdu is many centuries older than Hindi, giving it temporal precedence.

In the introduction of this chapter, Professor Jain categorically rejected the temporal precedence of Urdu literature over Hindi. To demonstrate that Urdu is older than Hindi, I have cited various Hindi scholars who affirm that the Urdu language and its literature are much older, and that Hindi emerged much later. I will now quote another passage from Professor Jain's book that reveals his own contradictions. Despite his efforts to downplay the age of

Urdu, he ultimately concedes that Urdu literature has outpaced Hindi literature. He writes:

"Foreign Muslims neither brought Urdu nor Khari Boli with them. Hindus did not pay attention to Khari Boli. Muslims took an interest in it and enriched it by incorporating Arabic and Persian words, resulting in the Urdu literature of Khari Boli, which left Hindi far behind" (p. 158).

Does this statement not confirm the precedence of Urdu over Hindi? The truth is that the literary tradition of Urdu is much older, and in this way, Urdu has both historical precedence and a richer tradition compared to Hindi.

CHAPTER SIX

Hindi Imperialism and Urdu Language

In his book *One Language: Two Scripts, Two Literatures*, Professor Jain attempts to claim that Hindi is older than Urdu, asserting that Khari Boli Hindi emerged around 1100 AD. However, this is completely inaccurate. The emergence of Khari Boli Hindi, also referred to as "Nagari Hindi" or Modern Hindi, actually began in the early 19th century when Lallu Lal Ji composed *Prem Sagar* at Fort William College in Calcutta. In this book, Professor Jain distorts both linguistic and historical facts.

Professor Jain's assertion that "Khari Boli Hindi is not just a single language, but a mixture of different languages of North India" (p. 15) reflects his lack of understanding of Indo-Aryan linguistics. He overlooks early dialects that emerged after 1000 AD in North India, such as Shor Seeni Apabhramsha and Magadhi Apabhramsha. Consequently, he lumps together dialects like Haryanvi, Braj Bhasha, Bundeli, Kanauji, Awadhi, Maithili, Bagheli, Chhattisgarhi, Bhojpuri, and Rajasthani under a single category. These dialects have never been mutually intelligible; otherwise, why would they be named differently? Each dialect is known for its unique regional characteristics. To group them all

62

under a single linguistic umbrella—particularly one like Khari Boli, which was relatively underdeveloped—is linguistic discrimination and an attempt to erase their linguistic identities and origins. Professor Jain's intention in doing so is to broaden the linguistic community of Hindi and create a larger Hindi-speaking majority. He writes:

"The speakers of these dialects happily consider themselves part of the Hindi brotherhood. Then why do Urdu speakers raise objections against this?"

Urdu speakers raise objections against this claim because they have historically protested this categorization. If Professor Jain disagrees, he should refer to the book *Language Movements in India,* published by CIIL Mysuru. One contributor, Baal Govind Mishra, offers a detailed account of the language movements in India. The organizers of these movements seek linguistic, cultural, and literary identity and expect their languages to develop independently. Many dialects have successfully had their demands recognized by the government.

The inclusion of 47 North Indian dialects (ranging from Haryana and Rajasthan to Bihar, Jharkhand, Madhya Pradesh, and Chhattisgarh) under the umbrella of "Hindi" is a clear example of Hindi imperialism. This classification has impacted the individuality of these dialects and dramatically inflated the number of reported Hindi speakers. According to the Census of India, these dialects are listed under Hindi, even though most have their own distinct linguistic structures, phonology, and lexicon, which differ significantly from Hindi. Some dialects even have established, authentic literary traditions. Of these, Maithili and Rajasthani have been recognized by the Sahitya Academy, and Maithili has been included in the curriculum of various universities in Bihar. However, Hindi has dominated to such an extent that these dialects struggle to assert their independence. Many Hindus have started movements to separate some of these dialects from Hindi. For example, based on their research, Jay Kant Mishra and Subhad Rajha have classified Maithili as a language distinct from Hindi. Similarly, Uday Narayan Tiwari considers Bhojpuri a separate language. Jay Narayan Vyas of Rajasthan initiated a strong movement to separate Rajasthani from Hindi. George Grierson also categorized Maithili, Bhojpuri, and Rajasthani as separate languages from Hindi. Suneeti Kumar Chatterjee recognized Maithili as an independent language and opposed its classification as a dialect of Hindi, arguing that Maithili has its own literature and unique linguistic characteristics. Uday Narayan Singh, the former director of CIIL, extensively discussed the historical and literary significance of Maithili in his article "*The Maithili Language Movements.*" However, despite the efforts of these intellectuals, their attempts were ultimately unsuccessful, and the dominance of Hindi persisted.

Hindi speakers fear that if dialects are granted language status, the Hindi-speaking community will shrink in terms of its total number of speakers. It is worth noting that according to the 1991 census, the total number of Hindi speakers was 337,272,114, constituting 39.85% of India's population. This number includes 47 dialects and other varieties of Hindi. If these dialects were not counted as part of Hindi, the actual number of Hindi speakers would have been reduced to 233,432,285, but the remaining 103,839,829 speakers would have maintained their linguistic and individual identities, as they had marked their dialects as their mother tongue in the census. This represents linguistic imperialism, where these dialects have been merged with Hindi, inflating the number of Hindi speakers. According to the 1991 census data, the Hindi-speaking population was reported as 39.85% of the total population. However, if we separate out the 47 dialects and other varieties, which account for 12.02% of the population, the actual percentage of Hindi speakers would drop to 27.83%.

If the dialects mentioned were allowed to grow independently, many of them, such as Awadhi, Maithili, Bhojpuri, Magahi, Braj Bhasha, Rajasthani, Mewati, Bagheli, Chhattisgarhi, Haryanvi, Garhwali, and Mewari, could evolve into distinct Indo-Aryan languages, much like Khari Boli did. Khari Boli, which originated from Shauraseni Apabhramsha after 1000 AD, was once an underdeveloped dialect but later developed into a language after being adopted by Muslims. This very language, in its cultural and refined form, is now known as Urdu, with earlier names such as Hindi, *Hindvi*, and Rekhta. Professor Jain is against this linguistic fact. He writes:

"Khari Boli Hindi (only Khari Boli) is probably an underdeveloped language (dialect). Under the leadership of foreign Muslims, it developed and took the shape of an interesting and literary language" (p. 16).

Professor Jain's perspective on Urdu seems heavily influenced by his biases. In his book, he views Urdu through the lens of Hindi speakers, particularly figures like Amrit Rai. According to Professor Jain, Amrit Rai boldly wrote against Urdu and identified himself as a loyal writer (p. 14).

Despite Jain's personal opinions, the linguistic reality is that Khari Boli Hindi, once an underdeveloped dialect, evolved into a fully-fledged language under the influence of Muslim leaders.

It is clear that Professor Jain has unfairly implicated Urdu literature and Muslims in the development of Hindi, suggesting they are solely responsible for its evolution. However, it is important to recognize that the linguistic movements related to these dialects in the Hindi region were led by non-Urdu speakers. They do not wish to integrate with the 'larger Hindi community', yet Professor Jain unjustly places the blame on 'Urdu speakers'.

Professor Jain has presented the linguistic dynamics of Urdu and Hindi in a biased manner, consistently favoring 'Hindi speakers'. Despite being a prominent Urdu linguist, he disagrees with nearly all perspectives presented by Urdu speakers. He distorts facts and draws inaccurate conclusions to support the dominance of Hindi. Regarding Hindi imperialism, Professor Jain himself admits that "Hindi speakers, with their imperialistic attitudes, have suppressed other languages through their writings" (p. 43).

Urdu, an independent, developed, and standard language, has unfortunately become a victim of Hindi imperialism. The Hindi circle, allegedly disregarding the rich literary and linguistic history of Urdu, labeled it as merely a style of Hindi due to their narrow-mindedness and linguistic bias. This decision was aimed at expanding the influence of Hindi. Linguistically, "style" refers to a particular manner of expression within a language. To reduce an independent, fully developed, and standard language to the status of a "style" of another language is to deny its existence and undermine its linguistic uniqueness. Such a classification leads to the gradual erosion of its literary and linguistic resources. It is ironic that Urdu, which is historically older than Khari Boli Hindi and richer from a literary perspective, is diminished by being labeled merely a style of Hindi. In reality, Urdu is on equal footing with Hindi and not a subordinate style. If one language were to be considered a style of the other, it would be Hindi, which originated from Khari Boli—the same linguistic source as Urdu. From this viewpoint, Hindi could be seen as a style of Urdu, not the reverse. The argument of the Hindi circle is unfounded.

The practice of referring to Urdu as a style of Hindi began in the second half of the nineteenth century when Ayodhya Prasad Khatri, a scholar of Khari Boli Hindi, classified Urdu as a style of Hindi. He failed to acknowledge the distinct characteristics and individuality of the two languages. According to Khatri, the only difference between Urdu and Hindi was the script. He proposed that the Urdu-speaking community adopt the Devanagari script instead of the Perso-Arabic script, and this notion was embraced by other Hindi scholars. To this day, many scholars, even outside the Hindi circle, refer to Urdu as a style of Hindi. Scholars like S.K. Chatterjee persist in calling it a style due to their narrow perspectives and communal biases.

Urdu is one of the languages listed in the Eighth Schedule of the Indian Constitution, granting it the same constitutional status as other languages. Consequently, the language census treats Urdu separately, just as it does with other scheduled languages in India. Had Urdu not been granted constitutional language status, it would not have been counted separately in the language census; instead, it would have been lumped together with Hindi. This is evident from the 1991 language census, in which forty-seven dialects from Northern India with ten crore speakers were integrated with Hindi speakers.

Professor Jain, who once acknowledged Hindi and Urdu as independent languages, now takes issue with their separate mention in the Constitution. He argues that this distinction is a "political strategy." In one of his articles, "Urdu, Hindi or Hindustani" (*Matbooa Hindustani Zubaan*, Mumbai, October 1973), Professor Jain states:

"The mention of Urdu and Hindi as independent languages in the Constitution of India is not a linguistic fact, but rather a political strategy."

Professor Jain argues that if Hindi is already mentioned in the Indian Constitution, there is no need to include Urdu as a separate language, as he believes Hindi and Urdu are essentially one language. While it is true that Hindi and Urdu are quite similar at the grassroots level, this is not the only factor that defines the uniqueness of a language. The true essence of a language is observed at higher levels, such as its literary, scientific, cultural, and functional dimensions. These qualities emerge after a language undergoes various stages of evolution, eventually becoming an independent, developed, and standard language. Urdu, being an independent and fully developed language, meets these criteria. However, Professor Jain disregards these higher levels and instead focuses solely on the grassroots level, emphasizing that "Hindi and Urdu are not two different languages" (p. 12).

While no linguist denies the similarities between Hindi and Urdu at the grassroots level, they are fundamentally different at higher levels—literary, scientific, cultural, and functional. Although they may overlap at the basic level, making it difficult to differentiate between them, these languages diverge significantly at more complex levels of analysis. This is why Hindi and Urdu cannot be considered the same language. As one examines their highest forms, the differences between the two languages become increasingly evident. It is likely for this reason that the framers of the Indian Constitution listed both languages separately in the Eighth Schedule. Yet, Professor Jain dismisses this fact, labeling it a "political strategy."

Though Hindi and Urdu share countless similarities, there are also distinct differences in pronunciation, proverbs, idiomatic expressions, morphology (including gender and number), particles, and other syntactic structures. The two languages also differ in their literary traditions, *talmihaat* and *isharat* (allusions and metaphors), poetry, rhyme schemes, literary trends, historical and cultural nuances, and the sources of their scientific and literary terminology. Moreover, Hindi and Urdu are written in different scripts. From a literary and cultural standpoint, it is clear that these languages are not one, despite their similarities from a descriptive linguistic perspective. Descriptive linguistics focuses solely on the structure and description of language, without accounting for the social and cultural contexts—a type of study referred to as asocial.

However, every language grows within its cultural and societal context. No language can be studied in isolation from its society, culture, and speakers. Therefore, languages must be examined not only from a structural and descriptive perspective but also from a sociocultural viewpoint, in a field known as sociolinguistics. Sociolinguistics studies speech communities, language identity, and the social and cultural functions of language.

Although Urdu and Hindi originated from the same linguistic source and are similar in structure and description, they have evolved in entirely different ways, particularly in their social, cultural, historical, and literary dimensions. This is why they cannot be considered a single language from a sociolinguistic perspective. Furthermore, the clear differences in their literary traditions, scientific and literary lexicon, and writing systems reinforce that these are two distinct languages. Beyond their shared grammatical structures, Hindi and Urdu differ significantly in pronunciation, daily idiomatic expressions and proverbs, old sayings, compound words, prefixes, suffixes, and markers for number and gender. Thus, there is no reason to treat them as one language.

Half a century ago, the renowned writer and intellectual Sajad Zaheer highlighted the differences between Urdu and Hindi not only in their literary and written forms but also in their cultural aspects. He stated that Urdu and Hindi are two distinct languages on a cultural level. In his book, Urdu, Hindi, Hindustani (Bombay: Kitaab Publishers; 1947), he writes:

"Urdu and Hindi differ in their modern literature and writing systems, despite their structural similarities. The most fundamental reason for this difference is cultural".
(P.40)

He further notes:

"Indian culture varies across regions while sharing many commonalities. However, in the areas where Urdu and Hindi are spoken, the divergence is marked by the differing cultural influences of Hinduism and Islam".

It is unfortunate that Sajad Zaheer's observation has not received due attention from the Urdu-speaking community, many of whom have accepted the notion that Urdu and Hindi are the same language. Dr. Kamal Ahmad Siddiqui echoes Professor Jain's sentiment, writing: "I completely agree with Professor Jain's statement that Urdu and Hindi are one language" (*One Language...*, p. 9).

Professor Jain maintains that Urdu and Hindi are not separate languages but associates Urdu with Muslim identity and Hindi with Hindu identity from a cultural perspective. He writes,

"Whether one agrees or not, the fact remains that from a cultural standpoint, the identity that Muslims portray through Urdu language and literature is absent in Hindi. Similarly, the identity markers that Hindus project through Hindi are not present in Urdu. The linguistic and cultural background of Urdu language and literature is rooted in Arabic and Islam, while Hindi leans towards Hinduism and Sanskrit" (*One Language...*, p. 279).

Professor Jain acknowledges that Urdu and Hindi exhibit differences from a religious and cultural perspective. So why does he refuse to accept that Urdu and Hindi are, in fact, two distinct languages? The similarities in origin, structure, and grassroots-level usage do not change this fundamental reality. Even if some try to prove that Urdu and Hindi are one language, the undeniable truth is that, at a cultural level, due to their religious and cultural idiosyncrasies, Urdu and Hindi are two different languages.

I accept that language is not inherently tied to religion or culture, and that Urdu is not solely a language for Muslims, nor do all Muslims in India speak Urdu. However, I cannot overlook the fact that Urdu is primarily spoken by Muslims, and for this reason, it has been significantly influenced by Muslim culture, becoming an identity marker for Muslims in India. Similarly, Hindi has become an identity marker for Hindus. There is no issue in acknowledging this reality in a democratic and secular nation like India. If the only differences between Urdu and Hindi are cultural and religious, and no other distinctions can be found, the fault does not lie with the languages themselves but with our limited vision.

Urdu, a modified form of Khari Boli, originated in the 12th century in Delhi and New Delhi. It became the foundation for the later development of Khari Boli Hindi, which was initially used for prose but evolved into a poetic language by the 20th century. This is how Khari Boli Hindi, now known as modern Hindi, originated after Urdu. This linguistic fact is supported by scholars like Dharendra Verma (author of *Politics of Hindi*) and other Hindu and Christian scholars such as Bashmol Kar and Steve Faraar (authors of *One Language, Two Scripts*). The divergence between these two languages became evident in the 19th century when Urdu continued using its script, while Khari Boli Hindi adopted the Devanagari script, earning the name "Nagari Hindi." Hindi also came to be known as "Standard Hindi." It drew its vocabulary and scientific terminology from Sanskrit. From literary, social, historical, and cultural perspectives, Hindi and Urdu became distinct languages, and even today, they remain so. Therefore, it is inaccurate to call Urdu and Hindi the same language—whether from a literary, scientific, social, cultural, or even a sociolinguistic perspective. It has been centuries since Urdu and Hindi took separate paths. In the contemporary linguistic scenario of India, It is not the realistic way to consider these languages as one!

The Urdu-speaking community should assert that Urdu and Hindi are two distinct languages, not merely that Urdu is a style of Hindi, but that they are linguistic equals. Both languages possess their own unique linguistic features, literary traditions, and cultural values. Each has its own individual identity, and both languages are spoken by large populations in India. Both are among India's major languages. In terms of the number of speakers, Hindi is the most spoken language in India, with Urdu ranking sixth. According to the 1991 Census, 13.5% of India's population, or 43,406,932 people, spoke Urdu. This makes it a more widely spoken language than several others listed in the Eighth Schedule of the Indian Constitution, including Gujarati, Kannada, Oriya, Punjabi, Kashmiri, and Sindhi. The linguistic identities of Urdu and Hindi speakers are distinct, giving rise to two separate speech communities. All these factors confirm that Urdu and Hindi are independent, distinct, and standardized languages.

It is important to note that the Hindi-speaking community has, from the outset, claimed that Urdu and Hindi are the same language, insisting that both should share the same script—Devanagari. In response to this dangerous trend, the Urdu community must take a stand and firmly assert that Urdu and Hindi are two separate languages, and therefore, their scripts must remain distinct. The current script of Urdu is indispensable for its survival. If the Urdu community does not defend the separate and independent status of Urdu from Hindi, scholars like Professor Jain and others within the Hindi circle will continue to argue that Urdu and Hindi are one language. While this will not affect Hindi, however,

Urdu like many other dialects and languages in India, may fall victim to "Hindi imperialism".

CHAPTER SEVEN

The Outcome of *Prem Sagar*

Professor Jain discusses *Prem Sagar* by Lalluji Ram in great detail. In the preface of *Prem Sagar*, it is mentioned:

"In 1803, Chittar Baj Mishar translated the tenth Skandh of the *Shrimat Bhagwat* into Braj Basha for Hindu schools, at the behest of John Gilchrist. Lalluji Lal then abandoned the Yamini language and wrote *Prem Sagar* in the city dialect of Delhi and Agra's Braj Basha" (*Movement of Khari Boli* by Shrikanth Mishar, p. 2).

Here are six key points about this excerpt:

1. *Prem Sagar* was written in Hindi, but it was not Lalluji Lal's original work.
2. Lalluji Lal claimed to have abandoned the "Yamini language" when writing this story.
3. He called the language of the story "Khari Boli of Delhi and Agra," not Hindi or Khari Boli Hindi, because at the time, "Hindi" referred to Urdu.
4. Before *Prem Sagar*, Braj Basha was traditionally used for poetry. Chattar Bhaj Mishar had translated the tenth Skandh of the *Shrimat Bhagwat* into Braj

Basha for Hindu schools, following John Gilchrist's request.

5. Prior to *Prem Sagar*, Khari Boli lacked a tradition of prose or poetry. There was no book in Khari Boli that could be used in schools, which is why Lalluji Lal wrote this prose in Khari Boli.

6. Lalluji Lal wrote *Prem Sagar* under the direction of John Gilchrist from Fort William College.

Lalluji Lal claimed that while writing *Prem Sagar*, he rejected the "Yamini language" and instead used "Khari Boli of Delhi and Agra." By "Yamini Basha," Lalluji Lal referred to the language of Muslims, which includes words from Indo-Aryan languages such as Arabic and Persian. This language, based on Khari Boli, developed around Delhi in the 12th century. Initially called Hindi, *Hindvi*, or Rekhta, it later became known as Urdu. Essentially, the Yamini language and Lalluji Lal's Khari Boli were the same at their core. The difference was that Yamini included Arabic and Persian words, whereas Lalluji Lal's Khari Boli excluded them. The so-called "Yamini language" was, in fact, Urdu. By replacing the Arabic and Persian vocabulary, Lalluji Lal created a style that he called the "Khari Boli of Delhi-Agra." According to renowned Hindi researcher Shitti Kanth Mishra:

"The Khari Boli of Delhi-Agra is one of the religious styles, which is devoid of Arabic and Persian lexicon and is purely a style of Hindustani."

Shitti Kanth Mishra points out that Lalluji Lal's "Khari Boli of Delhi-Agra" is a religious variant of Hindustani, devoid of Arabic and Persian lexicon. This clarification confirms that by the time *Prem Sagar* was written, Urdu had already evolved into an independent, developed language. Hindustani refers to none other than Urdu, and Khari Boli was essentially an adaptation of Urdu without Arabic and Persian influences. Mishra calls this style the "Pure Hindustani Style," achieved by excluding Arabic and Persian words.

This fact needs no further explanation. By the time *Prem Sagar* was created in 1803, the Yamini language (what Hindus referred to as the language of Muslims) was already well established, indicating that Urdu existed. This is why Lalluji Lal emphasized that he wrote *Prem Sagar* in the "Khari Boli of Delhi-Agra," excluding the Yamini language. Lalluji Lal, proficient in Urdu, collaborated with Mirza Qazim Ali Jawaan and Mazhar Ali Khan Wala at Fort William College to write books like *Sakuntala Natak*, *Shanghas Bateesi*, and *Betaal Pacheesi*. Thus, it was easy for him to omit Arabic and Persian words while composing *Prem Sagar* in Khari Boli. Lalluji Lal referred to it as the Yamini language because of the presence of Arabic and Persian words. In his book *One Language, Two Scripts*, Christopher King mentions that Lalluji Lal intentionally excluded words from languages associated with Muslims, such as Arabic, Persian, and Turkish (p. 27).

George Grierson and other scholars have made similar observations. It is undeniable that Arabic and Persian words were deliberately excluded from *Prem Sagar* in Khari Boli for religious reasons. However, Professor Jain disagrees (*One Language...*, pp. 16), suggesting instead that Lalluji Lal avoided using Muslim-associated languages because he was writing a book on Hinduism (p. 127). This contradiction in Professor Jain's argument is quite apparent.

To support the notion of Hindi's historical and linguistic superiority over Urdu, Professor Jain stretches his argument too far. He claims that

"Various versions of prose" can be traced back to earlier periods in Khari Boli Hindi" (p. 300).

He then criticizes the Urdu community, calling them "narrow-minded critics" for believing that *Prem Sagar* was the first Hindi prose work in the 19th century, asserting that they are unaware of King Koyi's journal, *Chand Chhand Barnan ki Mehma*, which he claims was the certified model for Khari Boli Hindi during Akbar's reign (1556-1605).

"The narrow-minded critics of Urdu, who consider the 19th-century book *Prem Sagar* as the first prose of Hindi, will be surprised to know that they are unaware of King Koyi's famous journals" (p. 103).

Professor Jain expresses surprise that the Urdu community was unfamiliar with King Koyi's journal, yet he himself seems unaware that Hindi scholars had declared it unauthentic fifty years ago. Even today, Professor Jain considers it an authentic source, which is perplexing. In his renowned work *The Khari Boli Movement*, Dr. Shatti Kanth Mishra, a prominent Hindi scholar and former head of the Department of Hindi at BHU, writes:

"The writings of King and Jatmal have been proven unauthentic" (p. 62).

Mishra's book, published in 1954 by *Nagri Parcharni Sabha* in Banaras, is a certified work on Khari Boli in northern India. It is astonishing that a scholar of Professor Jain's stature was unaware of this book. Despite conducting extensive research on Hindi literature and exchanging thoughts with eminent scholars like Amrit Rai, Professor Jain seems to have missed the fact that Hindi scholars themselves declared King Koyi's journal unauthentic. Nevertheless, Professor Jain uses Shatti Kant Mishra's book as a certified reference for Khari Boli Hindi (*One Language...*, p. 300) to argue Hindi's historical precedence over Urdu. This undermines the credibility of his research. Professor Jain should know better than to base his argument on such questionable foundations.

It is difficult to find a scholar as careless as Professor Jain in the field of endangered languages who would openly admit, "I have not conducted any personal research; I am just copying." In the introduction of his book, Professor Jain writes:

"I accept the fact that I have not done any personal research on Hindi articles. I am just copying them" (p. 301).

As the saying goes, even copying requires skill! If Professor Jain had applied his intellect, he would not have included unauthentic sources for Khari Boli Hindi. If he hasn't done any research by his own on primary sources, what was the need to write such an extensive book and make such grand claims?

In *One Language...*, Professor Jain refers to *Chand Chhand Barnan ki Mehma* multiple times, calling it the "First Prose Book of Khari Boli Hindi" (p. 129). Unfortunately, Professor Jain remains unaware that this book was proven unauthentic by the Hindi community fifty years ago.

Lalluji Lal referred to the Khari Boli of *Prem Sagar* as the "Khari Boli of Delhi and Agra" because, after Delhi, Agra served as India's capital from the reign of Sikander Lodhi to Shah Jahan, until 1647. During this time, Khari Boli speakers, or Urdu speakers, had migrated to Agra. Although Braj Bhasha was the dominant language of Agra, the city became a center for Urdu or Khari Boli, and Urdu came to be known as the language of Agra, as well as Delhi.

Another significant fact is that Gilchrist urged Lalluji Lal to write *Prem Sagar* to create a distinct language for Hindus that would serve their religious and educational needs.

Lalluji Lal accomplished this task well. He named *Prem Sagar* after the story from the *Shrimat Bhagwat's* tenth Skhand, addressing the religious and educational needs of Hindus, as he wrote the book for Hindu schools. By abandoning the "Yamini language" and adopting a new linguistic style, Lalluji Lal's work gave rise to a new language, marking the linguistic split between Urdu and Hindi—whether Professor Jain or other Hindi scholars agree with it or not.

In his book *The Hindee Roman Orthoepical Ultimatum* (1804), Gilchrist praised Lalluji Lal's writing style, stating: "*Prem Sagar* is an interesting book written by Lalluji Lal to introduce Hindustani with the beauty and clarity of Braj Basha, keeping in mind the interests of the larger Hindu audience" (Mishar, 03).

This statement from Gilchrist demonstrates that he influenced Lalluji Lal to write *Prem Sagar* with the needs of Hindus in mind. Thus, we can conclude that *Prem Sagar* deviated from the educational policy of Fort William College, which was never established to promote religious books for any particular group. The primary objective of the college was to serve British interests in India by training British officials in Persian (the official language) and Urdu, which was widely spoken in India. Numerous books were written, published, and translated in Urdu. Lalluji Lal, however, sought to benefit Hindus by using the widely understood Urdu (a modified version of Khari Boli) while excluding Arabic and Persian words and adopting the Nagari script. This ultimately resulted in the emergence of a new linguistic structure for Hindus. Can this not be considered a linguistic division? Shouldn't Lalluji Lal be held responsible for this, as he carried out the task under Gilchrist's guidance?

It is undeniable that before the emergence of *Prem Sagar*, there was no concept of a "Yamini Language." Across northern India, there was one language that transcended religious boundaries, used by both Hindus and Muslims for communication and writing. This language, referred to as Urdu by the British and Hindustani by Gilchrist in *The Oriental Linguist*, was described as "The Popular Language of Hindustan." While regional dialects existed, their influence was limited. Urdu served as the lingua franca from North India to Punjab and Bihar, not only as a literary language but also as a medium of education and official discourse. This continued until the 19th century, as SK Chatterjee discusses in *Indo-Aryan and Hindi*, emphasizing Urdu's prominence among Hindus.

"The Hindus continued to cultivate Braj Bhakha and Awadhi, when they wrote poetry. But from the 19th century, Urdu claimed their chief attention, as the language of the law courts, and as the medium of instruction in the schools leading to the professions of law, medicine, engineering, etc. What restricted education was available in North India before the Universities were established was through Urdu. The Hindus also accepted this Urdu tradition at school and college from Panjab to Bihar, when they needed a workable prose in Hindustani." (Pp. 213-14)

"Enthusiasts for Nagari Hindi, i.e. Sanskritised Hindi written and printed in Nagari characters, ordinarily now have no idea about the origin and evolution of this kind of Hindi half a century ago. It was difficult to find a clerk in a law court in Panjab, U.P. and Bihar who could write a plaint or a deed in Nagari letters. Most educated Hindus read Urdu, although they were just taking a lukewarm interest in *Nagari pracar* or movement for the spread of Nagari Hindi in both the law courts and the schools." (Ibid., p. 215).

(Note: Chatterjee gave this lecture in Ahmedabad during 1940-1941, and it was subsequently published as a book titled Indo-Aryan and Hindi *by the Gujarat Vernacular Society in January 1942.)*

Lalluji Lal wrote *Prem Sagar* with the religious and educational needs of the Hindu community in mind. It was essential for him to exclude Arabic and Persian words and instead incorporate Sanskrit terms, which hold religious significance for Hindus. Professor Jain concurs that Lalluji Lal's work was intended as a religious text for Hinduism, which is why he avoided using Arabic and Persian vocabulary. As Professor Jain points out:

"Lalluji Lal was preparing a book for Hinduism; that's why he abstained from using Arabic and Persian words" (*One Language...*, p.127).

However, this exclusion of certain words led to a linguistic split and separatism, resulting in a language distinct from Urdu, for which the Devanagari script was adopted. This script had traditionally been used for Sanskrit and a few other regional dialects. In the 19th century, this linguistic divide and separatism were reinforced by various Hindu organizations, particularly the *Nagari Pracharini Sabha*. This movement evolved into a full-fledged linguistic campaign, heavily influenced by religious and nationalist sentiments. By around 1885, Hindi advocates had coined a slogan that encapsulated the essence of the Hindi Movement.

In *Indo-Aryan and Hindi*, SK Chatterjee sheds light on these developments:

"Hindus with a nationalistic or patriotic temperament and love for Sanskrit, began to turn wistfully towards Sanskritic Hindi in Nagari characters. Support in this direction came from Bengal and Panjab (the *Arya Samaj*).... Slowly Hindus came to feel that there must be a revival of the Nagari Alphabet. The *Nagari Pracarini Sabha* was started at Banaras in 1890; and a new era ----- a veritable rebirth of Hindi ---came into being." (P. 214).

Garcin de Tassy's reviews of Indian languages and literature from 1870 provide additional insight into the widespread use of Urdu in northern India during the 19th century. He mentions various Urdu and Hindi newspapers, including the weekly Hindi paper *Jag Samachar*, which had recently been launched in Meerut. Based on de Tassy's description of its language, it is evident that Urdu was the lingua franca of the time, even playing an essential role in Hindi publications. De Tassy notes:

"No matter what anyone says, it is certain that Urdu is more widely used than other languages. Proof of this is also found in the fact that the most important advertisement in this

Hindi newspaper (*Jag Samachar*) is in Urdu in Persian script. The newspaper also makes it clear that its language is common, although it is in Nagari script. Therefore, in terms of language, this newspaper is in Urdu and not in Hindi" (De Tassy, p. 36).

It is a well-established fact that Lallu Lal, in the early 19th century, wrote *Prem Sagar* in the Indian subcontinent with the intention of creating a distinct language. However, this led to the division of speakers of a common language into two distinct groups, further promoting sectarianism and sparking the long-lasting linguistic conflict known as the Hindi-Urdu controversy.

CHAPTER EIGHT

Urdu, Hindi, Hindustani and The Fort William College

In his book *One Language, Two Scripts, Two Literatures*, Professor Jain extensively examines the linguistic divide and the Urdu-Hindi conflict in northern India during the 19th century. However, he places the entire blame on Urdu and Muslims, ignoring the propaganda against Khari Boli Hindi and the Devanagari script, as well as the anti-Urdu activities of revivalist organizations. Jain sides with the Hindi community, attributing all responsibility for the conflict to the Urdu circle.

Multiple sources confirm that in the 19th century, Khari Boli Hindi was deliberately pitted against Urdu on religious grounds. This period marked the rise of anti-Urdu sentiment and the emergence of Hindi movements, driven by aggressive efforts within the Hindu community to suppress the Urdu language and its script.

Modern Khari Boli Hindi has its roots in Khari Boli, which evolved into Urdu in northern India during the 12th century. Over time, Urdu acquired various names such as Hindi or *Hindvi, Rekhta, Zaban-e-Dehli* (or *Dehlivi*), *Dakani* (in the Deccan), Gujri (in Gujarat), and *Zaban-e-Hindustan*, as it was called by *Millawajihi* in *Sabras*. Despite these various names, it ultimately became known as Urdu. By this point, the language had become highly refined.

At the beginning of the 19th century, when Khari Boli Hindi began to emerge, Urdu had already developed into a refined literary language. Though still called *Hindvi*, Khari Boli was associated with Muslims from its inception. Consequently, many Hindus scorned it, referring to it as "Musalmani Basha" or "Maleechh Basha," and thus it wasn't widely embraced by Hindus for some time. It was only after Urdu gained prominence as the popular language of northern India and blossomed as a literary language that Hindus began to take note of it. However, Professor Jain argues that:

"It was only when the East India Company and the British government adopted first Persian, and then Urdu, in official matters that the Hindi community began to pay attention to Khari Boli" (p. 129).

This contradicts his earlier statement (p.15), where he posits that Khari Boli Hindi likely came into existence around 1100 AD. This raises the question: If Khari Boli Hindi existed in 1100 AD, why did the Hindi community only take notice of it in the 19th century, and why was it called Hindi? The word

"Hindi" is a Persian term, introduced by Muslims in the 12th century to describe the refined form of Khari Boli. This form, also known as Hindi, *Hindvi*, or Rekhta, became the earliest form of Urdu. To assert the historical dominance of Hindi over Urdu, Professor Jain seems to have forgotten what he previously stated in his own book (p. 129).Professor Jain's contradictory statements suggest that he is attempting to establish Khari Boli Hindi as having a history older than that of Urdu, despite knowing that the actual linguistic history is quite the opposite.

It is undeniable that prose examples of Khari Boli Hindi only appear from the mid-19th century, and poetic examples emerge in the 20th century. The prose works of Khari Boli Hindi published before the 19th century, which Jain mentions in his book, are either unauthentic or belong to other languages like Braj Basha. For example, Keng Koyi's prose journals *Chand Chhand Barnan ki Mehma*, written during Akbar's reign (1605-1886), were proven to be unauthentic by the Hindi community itself. Yet, Professor Jain considers them authentic (p. 300).

Although the poetic tradition of Khari Boli Hindi began in the 20th century, the movement advocating for it started in the late 19th century. Ayodhiya Prasad Khatri, from

Muzaffarpur, Bihar, was a key figure in this movement. He advocated for Khari Boli Hindi to be used not only for prose but also for poetry. After 1837, in northern India, Urdu, with its Perso-Arabic script, was accepted as the official language, used in courts, offices, and education. Khatri admired Urdu for its structural resemblance to Khari Boli, but he saw the script as the only difference between Urdu and Hindi. While familiar with Urdu, he was unfamiliar with the Persian script. Khatri encouraged the Urdu community to adopt the Devanagari script instead of the Perso-Arabic one. One of the supporters of Khari Boli Hindi poetry was Shri Dhar Pathak, who had numerous debates with advocates of Braj Basha. On the opposing side were Radha Charan Gowsami and Pratap Narayan Mishar, who believed that Braj Basha was superior to Khari Boli and more suitable for poetry. However, as Urdu expanded and gained wider acceptance, Khari Boli Hindi also grew in prominence, and by the 20th century, Braj Basha began to decline. Eventually, Hindus began to accept Khari Boli Hindi for poetry as well. Professor Jain observes that:

"Khari Boli came into the limelight substantially at the beginning of the 20th century. Mahavir Prasad Divedi, Pandit BN Bhat, and M. S. Gupt supported it. In 1912, Babu Sham Sundar Das wrote to the Uttar Pradesh Department of

Education, requesting that Braj Basha elements be excluded from Hindi books. In 1914, Maithili Charan Gupt argued in one of the conferences of *Hindi Sahitiya Sameelan* that supporters of Braj Basha are enemies of the national language Hindi" (p. 182).

Professor Jain refers to the controversy between Khari Boli Hindi and Braj Basha as an "internal conflict," claiming that it is purely a matter for the Hindi community and has nothing to do with the Urdu circle" (p. 174).Whether Professor Jain considers it relevant or not, this "internal conflict" is of significant interest to the Urdu community because it helps trace the literary origins of Khari Boli and undermines Professor Jain's claim that Hindi predates Urdu.

In the early 19th century, an anti-Urdu ideology began to take shape with the emergence of Khari Boli Hindi. This stemmed from the efforts of Lalluji Lal at Fort William College in Calcutta, who removed Arabic and Persian words from Urdu in an attempt to create a new language driven by religious discrimination and communalism. This was essentially the result of Gilchrist's anti-Urdu agenda, which was perpetuated by Western forces and gave rise to the Hindi-Urdu conflict.

On the recommendation of Dr. John Gilchrist, Head of the Hindustani Department at Fort William College, Lalluji Lal was appointed as *Bhakha Munshi* on June 7th, 1802, with a monthly salary of Rs.50. His primary responsibility was to teach *Bhakha* to *Munshis* unfamiliar with the language. However, Gilchrist assigned Lal additional tasks, and in 1803, under Gilchrist's direction, Lalluji Lal wrote *Prem Sagar*. Although Gilchrist made significant contributions to the Urdu language and literature, he also played a role in sparking the Urdu-Hindi conflict. Under his supervision, the Fort William College campus saw the development of a new language called Khari Boli Hindi. Eventually, Lalluji Lal and Munshi Sadal Misher from Fort William College began writing Khari Boli in the Devanagari script, replacing Arabic and Persian words with Sanskrit. Suniti Kumar Chatterjee referred to this language as Sanskritized Hindi. Chatterjee notes:

> "Hindus with a nationalist or patriotic temperament and love for Sanskrit, began to turn wistfully towards Sanskritic Hindi in Nagari characters." (*Indo-Aryan and Hindi*, p. 214).

Looking at the nineteenth century from an external perspective, it seems marked by anti-Urdu sentiments and communal animosity. From July 10, 1800, when Governor-General Marquess Wellesley established Fort William College, to April 18, 1900, when Lieutenant Governor Sir Antony Macdonald ordered the use of Nagari script in the courts and government offices of the north-western regions and Awadh, the Urdu language and script faced intense opposition from both the Hindu community and the British government.

When Lalluji Lal created a new language using Urdu material at Fort William College, the elites of "Yamini Basha" named it "Delhi Agra's Khari Boli" and adopted the Nagari or Devanagari script for it. They didn't call it Hindi, Hindustani, or Rekhta, as those names were exclusively used for Urdu. The word "Urdu" had just come into existence. To distinguish this new language from Hindi, Hindustani, Rekhta, and Urdu, it was called *Bhakha*. Lalluji Lal was appointed *Bhakha Munshi* at Fort William College, where Braj Bhasha gained prominence among Hindus due to its association with devotion to Lord Krishna and its rich poetic tradition. Hindu intellectuals of the time believed that Khari Boli Hindi was derived from Braj Bhasha. However, it is undeniable that Braj Bhasha dominated Hindi for a long time.

Gilchrist resigned from the Fort William College in February 1804, but the seeds of the Hindi-Urdu conflict that he sowed continued to grow. His followers and successors harbored ongoing resentment toward Urdu. In 1808, William Taylor was appointed professor and head of the Hindustani Department at Fort William College. It is said that William Taylor was the first to use the word "Hindi" for Khari Boli Hindi, written in the present-day Devanagari script, whereas the word "Hindi" had been used for the popular language written in Persian script, which is modern Urdu, also called Hindustani by Fort William College members and other English people until the end of the nineteenth century.

In 1812, William Taylor presented a report to the Fort William College council, where he used the term "Hindi" in a modern context. The report states:

"I am only referring to Hindustani or Rekhta, written in the Persian script. I am not referring to Hindi, which has its own script, or the language that excludes Arabic and Persian lexicon." (Laxashmi Sagar Varshini, *Fort William College*, Shri Kant Misher, *Khari Boli Movement*, p. 71).

In 1803, the language created by Lalluji Lal at Fort William College was named "Hindi with its own script" in 1812 on the same campus.

After the retirement of William Taylor, William Paries became the professor and head of the department of Hindustani in 1823. He was a strong supporter of Hindi and favored it over Urdu. His preference for Hindi was reflected in his title as the professor of Hindustani, which he referred to as Hindi. During the same period, Lieutenant D-Radal was appointed as the secretary of the Fort William College council. Prior to this, he worked as an examiner and was also against Urdu, considering it a foreign language brought by the Mughals, and he preferred an indigenous language. A letter he wrote to the Law Secretary on behalf of the college council on September 24, 1824, clearly reflects his disdain for Urdu. An excerpt is provided below:

"Hindustani, also referred to as Urdu, is spoken by the elites of India, particularly Muslims. Since it was brought by the Mughals, it is still considered a foreign language. Even after receiving basic education in Urdu, three-fourths of the population do not understand its Arabic and Persian lexicon. Instead, any indigenous language derived from Sanskrit would be more productive." (Prof Jain, *One Language...*, p. 165).

This paragraph clearly demonstrates Lieutenant D-Radal's lack of understanding and misinformation about Urdu, as well as his hatred toward the language.

Subsequent events of the Fort William College council suggest that they had started a movement against Urdu. On the recommendation of the college council, the Governor-General ordered that newly appointed East India Company employees be educated in Braj Bhasha instead of Hindustani. According to Professor Jain, the Governor-General approved this suggestion. (ibid).

In his book *Linguistic Conflict* (1997), Professor Beg stated that: "Not only Fort William College but also the British government was against the Urdu language" (p. 254).

However, Professor Jain took offense to this statement and criticized the author in his book (p. 123).

Professor Jain's criticism seems unfounded, as he ignored Hukum Chand Nair's statement in his book *Issues of Urdu* (1977). Nair explicitly held the authorities of Fort William

College responsible for creating Khari Boli Hindi and also mentioned the British government's interest in promoting Hindi as the national, cultural, and common language of Hindus. Nair explains:

"Although the authorities of Fort William College published many Urdu books in Devanagari script at the beginning of the 19th century and laid the foundation of Pure Hindi based on Khari Boli by getting Lalluji Lal to write *Prem Sagar* (The Ocean of Love), in the middle of this century, Devanagari and Hindi were limited to within the walls of Fort William College or only in the minds of European authorities. During this era, British authorities made every effort to make Hindi the national, cultural, and common language of Hindus, as can be seen from the report of JR Balentine, who was the head of the Department of English and the Principal of Banaras College (formerly Sanskrit College and later Koinis College)" (p. 85-86).

Afterward, Hukum Chand Nair presented an outline of Balentine's report, which clearly indicated that he was encouraging Hindu students (who had no interest in Hindi) to study Hindi and consider it the language of their mothers and sisters. He asked his students to write an essay titled "Why do you consider the daily language and culture of your mothers and sisters inferior?" The students were surprised and submitted a memorandum to Balentine, questioning, "Why do you think this way?" The students even stated, "We do not understand why you (Europeans) consider only Hindi important when there are hundreds of dialects that, in our opinion, are equally valuable as Hindi" (*Linguistic Issues*, p. 87).

These reports clearly establish that during the first half of the 19th century, Hindi was given more importance and status than Urdu, and the British government supported Hindi over Urdu to create division and disrupt linguistic harmony between the two communities. This would have greatly benefited the British administration. It was not just Balentine but other English officials who also disliked Urdu and were always ready to promote Hindi. Sir Abraham Grierson, a renowned linguist from the Bengal Civil Service, gained fame for his *Linguistic Survey of India* and was also a strong advocate of the Hindi language. He was a member of the *Nagari Prachar Sabha*, which was established in Banaras in 1893 to promote Hindi and the Nagari script. According to Hukum Chand Nair, Grierson played a significant role in Macdonald's April 18, 1900 decision to make Hindi equal to Urdu in the offices and courts of the north-western provinces (ibid., p. 88).

Shaam Sundar Das, one of the founders of the *Nagari Pracharni Sabha*, writes in his autobiography '*My Own Story*' that he asked Grierson to publish an article in support of Hindi in any newspaper. When Grierson did not respond, Shaam Sundar Das wrote him a letter of complaint. Soon after, Macdonald's decision was made public, and Grierson wrote to Shaam Sundar, stating that everything he had done behind the scenes for Hindi could not have been accomplished by simply publishing an article (*Hukum Chand Nair*, p. 88).

In his book *One Language*, Professor Jain quotes Christopher King, stating that "there was no separate department of Hindi, whereas Hindustani, Arabic, and Persian already existed" (p. 166). However, King and Professor Jain should be aware that there was no need for a separate Hindi department in Fort William College because, when the college was established in 1800, Hindi (Khari Boli Hindi) did not exist. It came into existence after the establishment of the college. At that time, many regional languages like Braj Basha, Awadhi, and Rajasthani existed, but Khari Boli Hindi did not. This is why, at the end of 1824, the Fort William College council recommended that newly recruited employees of the East India Company be educated in Braj Basha instead of Hindustani. If Khari Boli Hindi existed at that time, why would the college council recommend Braj Basha, and why would the Governor-General approve the suggestion?

In the early stages of Fort William College, Gilchrist recommended the title "Bhaka Munshi" instead of Hindi Munshi because Khari Boli Hindi did not exist at that time, and the word "Hindi" was exclusively used to refer to Urdu. Even the translators and writers of Fort William College referred to Hindi as Urdu. For instance, the Urdu translation of the Quran was referred to as the Hindi translation. Professor Jain also acknowledges that "Hindi" was one of the alternative names for Urdu. He notes:

"Up to the beginning of the 19th century, Hindi was used for Urdu" (p. 134).

Ample evidence supports the fact that throughout the 19th century, the word "Hindi" was also used alongside Urdu to refer to the Urdu language. Even in the early 20th century, Iqbal used the term Hindi to mean Urdu in his Masnavi *Israr-i-Khudi*.

During the 19th century, "Hindustani" undoubtedly and exclusively referred to Urdu. Furthermore, the language that the English called "Hindustani" was Urdu written in the Persian or Perso-Arabic script, which is still recognized today as Urdu's script. Dr. Satti Pal Anand mentioned in one of his essays, *Fort William College and Initial Dictionaries* (published in the *Urdu Newspaper* [Islamabad], January 7, 2007), that:

"The language referred to as Hindustani, without a doubt, had a Perso-Arabic script, not Devanagari".

Some Hindi proponents mistakenly believe that the English referred to Khari Boli Hindi (written in the Devanagari script) as Hindustani, distinct from Urdu. However, the English never referred to Khari Boli Hindi as Hindustani; they used the term *"Bhakha"* instead. The term *Bhakha* also referred to various other regional languages of North India.

As for the Devanagari script, it was well-known during this period that it was an unpopular and less commonly used script. During Gilchrist's tenure at Fort William College, of the 36 employees—accountants, translators, and writers—appointed in the Hindustani department (detailed by Mohammed Ateeq Sidique in his book *Gilchrist and His Reign* [pp. 175-177]), only one was a *Bhakha* accountant (Lalluji Lal), one was a Nagari writer (Kashi Raj), and only one was a Nagari calligrapher (Mahanand). All other employees, except for a few, were appointed for work related to Urdu, which was equated with Hindustani.

In the 19th century, the Nagari script was evidently regarded as less significant. This is further highlighted in the preface of Major Joseph Taylor's *A Dictionary, Hindustani and English*, which states:

"A knowledge of the Nagari character being comparatively of little use to the generality of Hindustani scholars, I have entirely discarded it." (Adapted from an article by Satya Pal Anand).

This dictionary presents all words in Urdu with their Roman pronunciation, and their English meanings are given in italics. The Nagari script is not used at all in this dictionary. For example:

- A ناقه (*naqu*), f. (from نوق): A she-camel.
- P ناگاه (*nagah*): Suddenly, unexpectedly, all at once, unawares.
- H بمیں (*humen*): To us. *Humeen*: We, ourselves.
- S هنس (*huns*), m.: A duck.

Note: A represents Arabic, P stands for Persian, H is Hindustani, and S is Sanskrit.

Prior to this, Gilchrist had published *A Dictionary, English and Hindustani* in two volumes (1786 and 1790), where the meaning of English words is first given in Roman script, followed by Urdu script, without the use of Nagari script. For example:

- **TO ABANDON:** h. *chhorna* (چھورنا), *teagna* (تیاگنا), tujna (تجنا). A. *turk kurna* (ترک کرنا).
- **ABANDONED:** a. *khalee* (خالی), h. *soona* (سونا), *oojar* (اوجار), p. *weeran* (ویران).

Note: h is Hindustani, a is Arabic, and P is Persian.

It is evident that the Nagari script was not widely popular and there was a shortage of Nagari letter writers in the courts and offices. Even when attempts were made to find such writers, they were scarce. As Professor Jain notes "in the courts and offices of UP, Urdu was highly dominant" (pp. 186). To address this, the *Nagari Pracharini Sabha* was established in Banaras in 1893. According to Hukum Chand:

> "To incorporate Hindi and Nagari in the courts, the *Sabha* reached out to lawyers and writers in various

cities, trying to employ salaried Nagari writers who would write applications in Nagari free of charge in every district court. In 1903, the first paid Nagari writer was appointed in the Banaras court" (*Issues of Urdu*, p. 129).

From these examples, it is clear that, until the late 18th century and throughout the 19th century, "Hindustani" was synonymous with Urdu, not Hindi. Thus, the language referred to as Hindustani was written in the Urdu script, not in Nagari.

It is undeniable that social and cultural factors influenced the development of Hindi. The Khari Boli dialect, from which Hindi was later derived, was considered inferior by Hindus and often referred to as "*Maleesh Bhasha*," or an inferior language. As a result, until the early 19th century, Hindus did not write prose or poetry in this dialect. The new Khari Boli Hindi saw the rise of prose in the early 19th century and poetry in the 20th century. Before the 19th century, the term "Hindi" was not used to describe this language, as it was exclusively reserved for Urdu. This raises the question of how the authorities at Fort William College could have established a separate Hindi department. If such a department existed, what would have been taught under the name "Hindi"? It was not widely used, and Khari Boli Hindi had no prose or poetry to offer. It was embarrassing for Hindi when, in 1801, Gilchrist published a *Marsiya* (a poem commemorating a martyr's death) by Urdu poet Abdullah Miskeen for Hindi students at Fort William College, written in Devanagari script. Other works, such as Mirza Qazim Ali Jawan's *Sanghasan Bateesi* and *Sakuntala Natak*, along with Mazhar Ali Khan's *Betaal Pacheesi* and *Madhonal*, were originally in Urdu and won awards. Under Gilchrist's guidance, these works were later transcribed into Devanagari script.

In contrast, Urdu was firmly established throughout North India, with its rich literary traditions in both prose and poetry, and it predominated over Hindi in every sphere. It was also widely understood in other regions. When Gilchrist published his fourth book, *The Oriental Linguist*, in 1798, he referred to Urdu as the "popular language of Hindustan." Consequently, educating the newly appointed officials of the East India Company in Urdu, which the English referred to as "Hindustani," became essential. To this end, Gilchrist, an expert in Hindustani (Urdu), established the Oriental Seminary in Calcutta in January 1799. This institution, created under the direction of then-Governor-General Lord Wellesley, lasted for a year and a half and laid the groundwork for the establishment of Fort William College in Calcutta on July 10, 1800. Wellesley was deeply concerned with educating the company's officials in both Persian, the official language, and Hindustani (Urdu). By the time the Oriental Seminary was founded, Gilchrist had already gained mastery over Urdu and had published a two-volume *English and Hindustani Dictionary*, as well as a *Grammar of the Hindustani Language*. His reputation as an Urdu and oriental language scholar quickly spread, and when Fort William College was established in 1800, Gilchrist was appointed as the professor and head of the Hindustani department.

As previously mentioned, the East India Company and Fort William College referred to Urdu as "Hindustani" because Urdu was considered the popular language of India. Thus, the department dealing with the teaching of Urdu at Fort William College was named the Hindustani Department. At this time, there was no Hindi (modern Hindi in Devanagari script) in comparison to Urdu, as Hindi had not yet emerged. The term "Hindi" was exclusively used to refer to Urdu. Regional languages were referred to by their own names or as "*Bhakha/Basha*." The accountants and scholars in Fort William College's Hindustani Department, all well-versed in Urdu, referred to the college as *Madrasai Hindi* and to the department as *Dividing Hindi* or *Dividing Hindvi*, often calling Gilchrist the "Hindi teacher."

In the prefaces of their translations and compilations, these scholars detailed their life stories and often mentioned Urdu using various terms such as *"Zaban-e-Urdu," "Urdu Maula,"* "Hindi," *"Hindvi," "Zaban-e-Hindi,"* and *"Zaban-e-Rekhta."* For instance, Mir Aman used phrases like "Reality of Urdu," "People of Urdu," and *"Ek Zabaan Urdu ki Muqarar huwi"* in *Baag-o-Bahar.* In *Gunj Khoobi*, he referred to the "language of Urdu-e-Maula," and in *Ikhlaaq-e-Hindi*, Mir Bahadur Ali Hussaini noted that he had translated Persian discourses into Rekhta, calling it the language of all, and titled it *Ikhlaaq-e-Hindi.* Similarly, when Hyder Baksh Hyderi translated *Touti Naama* from Persian to Urdu, he stated in the preface that proverbs and idioms from *Zaban-i-Hindi* were translated into *Urdu-e-Maula* and titled *Touta Kahani.* He also mentioned that, in translation, the Arabic letter ط, which is absent in Hindi, was replaced by the letter ت. Hyder Baksh Hyderi's other famous work, *Aarayish Mehfil*, was also translated from Persian into Rekhta on Gilchrist's orders. He mentioned that "on the orders of John Gilchrist, may his star continue to ascend…, it was translated into Rekhta from his own perspective and named as 'Aarayish Mehfil'." Among the writers at Fort

William College was Sher Ali Afsos, who authored *Baag-e-Urdu*. In the preface, he explains that the book was named *Baag-e-Urdu* because it showcased the beauty of Urdu poetry and prose. Furthermore, on Gilchrist's recommendation, a project was undertaken at Fort William College to translate the Quran into Urdu. Although fifty-six pages were printed, the project was halted after Gilchrist left. Many scholars participated in this translation project, including Mirza Qazim Ali Jawaan. In the preface to his translation, Jawaan referred to the Rekhta language and repeatedly mentioned the word "Hindi." For example: "If the Quran has been translated into Persian, why not into Hindi?." "If the words of Allah are in Hindi, the people of Hind will understand them better." "It is believed that books from Arabic and Persian were slowly translated into Hindi." Qazim Ali Jawaan also wrote *Sakuntala Natik* in Urdu, and in its preface, he mentions that he translated it into Rekhta on Gilchrist's orders, referring to Gilchrist as the "Hindi Teacher.

"Colonel Scott, who is a senior resident of Lucknow, upon the request of the Governor General in 1800s, many poets were appointed as employees of the East India Company and sent them to Calcutta. Among them, Akhtar also entered here, and had the honor of being in the service of Hindi teacher by John Gilchrist. The very next day, Gilchrist said very kindly and politely, "Translate Sakuntala Natak in your language." (According to Muhammad Atiq Siddiqui, *Gilchrist and its Era*, p. 204).

Though not employees of Fort William College, figures like Mirza Ali Lutf, Nihal Chand Lahori, and Basit Khan were commissioned by Gilchrist to write books for the Hindustani Department. Lutf composed *Gulshan-e-Hindi* in Urdu, based on the Persian work *Gulzar-e-Ibrahim*, aiming to educate newly arrived English officials. Nihal Chand Lahori translated *Taj al-Malook and Gul Bagawali* into Urdu, renaming it *Mazheb-e-Ishq*. In the preface, he wrote that this work was compiled in Hindi and titled *Mazheb-e-Ishq* during Wellesley's era. Similarly, Basit Khan in the preface of *Gulshan-e-Hind* writes "that by Bismillah, if such a text appears in Hindi writing or speech, then the word is not blasphemy.

From these historical facts, it is evident that the term "Hindi" referred to Urdu in the early 19th century, not the modern Hindi written in Nagari script. Two hundred years ago, "Hindi" was synonymous with Urdu and was also called Rekhta and Hindustani. Consequently, it would have been impossible for Fort William College to establish a department for modern Hindi when Urdu (then known as Hindi) was already well established. Gyan Chand Jain's assertion that there was no Hindi department at Fort William College is based on the modern linguistic understanding. Had he considered the historical context, he might not have made such a claim. In analyzing linguistic issues of any era, one must consider the cultural and historical context. Professor Jain, however, relied solely on the available sources at Fort William College and overlooked the broader socio-political context of that era. The British authorities recognized Urdu's cultural and social importance and utilized it to their advantage, making it the most prominent language in North India. Urdu was given unparalleled status in North India, leading to the establishment of a dedicated department for it at Fort William College, known as the Hindustani Department. During this period, Khari Boli Hindi had neither linguistic significance nor social relevance. Even by the mid-19th century, Hindu students at Banaras Sanskrit College (later Queen's College) avoided studying Hindi, and the college principal, Balentine, who was a fervent advocate of Hindi, struggled to encourage students to learn it. This incident, occurring 45 years after the founding of Fort William College, reveals the limited relevance of Hindi at the time of the college's establishment.

Around 1800, Northern India was home to various languages, each bearing distinct names. One such language was "*Bhakha*," derived from the Sanskrit word "Bhasha," meaning "tongue." *Bhakha* was used not only for Braj Basha (the language of Delhi's southwestern region, centered around Mathura) but also for other regional and local languages. Some scholars consider *Bhakha* to be an early stage of what is now known as Nagari Hindi. Therefore, during this period (the early 19th century), Nagari Hindi was largely referred to as *Bhakha*. It was neither a well-established nor significant language at the time. Musi Sada Sukh Lal, the author of *Sukh Sagar* in Khari Boli Hindi, was primarily an Urdu poet known as Niyaz. He captured the decline of *Bhakha's* usage in one verse:

"Rasm-o-Rivaaj Bhakha ka, Duniya se uth gaya."

Bhakha was a general linguistic term that could be applied to any regional language other than Urdu, Hindi, *Hindvi*, Rekhta, or Hindustani. Its significance waned as people shifted towards the more prestigious and developed language, Urdu, as evidenced by Niyaz's verse. However, on June 7, 1802, Gilchrist appointed a *Bhakha* Munshi in the Hindustani Department, which was essentially the Urdu Department. The *Bhakha* Munshi earned a salary of Rs. 50

per month. When Gilchrist resigned in February 1804, his successor suspended Lalu Ji Lal, the *Bhakha* Munshi, on June 11, 1804, deeming him unnecessary. This reflects the uncertain status of Hindi during this period, making the idea of a separate Hindi department at Fort William College seem unrealistic.Professor Jain should have considered why Lalu Ji Lal, initially deemed important, was suspended by the Fort William College authorities just two years later. Meanwhile, many Urdu authors, translators, and accountants, such as Sher Ali Afsos, Mirza Qazim Ali Jawan, Mazhar Ali Khan Wali, Mir Bahadur Ali Husaini, Mir Aman, Hyder Baksh Hyderi, Jaleel Ali Khan Ashiq, Mirza Mohammed Fitrat Lucknowi, Movlvi Hafeez-ud-Din, Murtaza Khan, Tasaduq Hussain, and Wajid Ali, were retained in their roles and continued their work. While Professor Jain mentions Lalu Ji Lal's appointment, he omits the suspension. Had he mentioned it, the reason would have highlighted the limited popularity and relevance of Hindi during that era. Before placing blame on the Fort William College authorities, Professor Jain should have recognized that 'the college maintained departments for Urdu, Arabic, and Persian but not for Hindi'.(p. 17). If the *Bhakha* Munshi was considered unnecessary, what grounds existed for establishing a Hindi department? Why would the college invest in an unpopular and less useful language, which was still in its infancy? Another point to note is that Gilchrist himself regarded Khari Boli Hindi as vulgar. He commissioned several books to be written in Devanagari Khari Boli and also transcribed numerous Hindustani (Urdu) books into the Devanagari script. Scholars generally agree that when Gilchrist referred to "Hindustani," he meant Urdu, which he termed the "Genuine Hindustani Style." In contrast, he referred to Devanagari Khari Boli as *"Hindvi"* and labeled it the "Vulgar or Hindvi Style."

Gilchrist's successors at Fort William College supported *Hindvi*, promoting it as "Hind," but outside the college, it remained largely ignored and unpopular for a considerable time. However, from the mid-19th century, Hindus began paying greater attention to it. As Professor Jain notes, "The linguistic issues arose after the revolt against the British... Hindu and Hindi started to grow" (p. 186). Professor Jain's book lacks evidence showing that the British and the East India Company actively supported the rise of Hindi or worked to establish it as the national and cultural identity of Hindus. However, from the establishment of Fort William College on July 10, 1800, to the decision on April 18, 1900, regarding the imposition of Nagari script, Professor Jain justifies every event that impacted Urdu by placing the blame on Muslims.

CHAPTER NINE

Anti-Urdu Movements and Tendencies

After Gilchrist left Fort William College in 1804, it became evident that his successors did not treat Urdu favorably. Outside the college, the British government adopted a strict stance towards Urdu, while aggressive campaigns and movements against the Urdu script by Hindus gained momentum. Hindu social and reform movements, along with revivalist groups, publicly opposed Urdu and promoted Sanskrit, Hindi, and the Nagari script. In many ways, the Hindi-Urdu conflict that gripped northern India was inflamed by sectarian sentiments and tendencies.

The Brahmo Samaj, a social reform movement in Bengal, played a pivotal role in promoting Hindi. In contrast, the Arya Samaj, a revivalist organization founded in Punjab in 1875, focused on reforming Hinduism and promoting the Hindi language. The Arya Samaj actively propagated Hindi through its teachings and publications. Led by Swami Dayanand Saraswati, the movement made it compulsory for its followers to learn Hindi. Shardha Ram Phaluri, another social activist from Punjab, openly criticized Urdu in his writings and speeches. This had a significant impact on the

Hindu community in Punjab, leading many to distance themselves from Urdu. Shati Kanth Mishra writes about Shardha Ram Phaluri:

"Through his speeches, the Hindu masses of Punjab learned to detach themselves from Muslim influences and the Urdu language, embracing the Hindi language and Hindu religion." (*Khari Boli Ka Andolan*, p. 94)

Lala Lajpat Rai, a prominent leader of the Arya Samaj, admitted that before joining the organization, he had little knowledge of Hindi. However, after becoming part of the Arya Samaj, he became actively involved in promoting the Hindi language in Punjab. The Arya Samaj created a divisive atmosphere in the region, planting seeds of prejudice against Urdu. This eventually led a significant number of Hindus in Punjab, who were previously familiar with Urdu, to shift their linguistic allegiance to Hindi.

In his book *One Language, Two Scripts* (p. 200), Professor Jain makes an unfounded claim by accusing Professor Jagannath Azad, a renowned Urdu poet and scholar of *Iqbaliyat*, of being an Arya Samaji. This accusation is entirely baseless, as Azad did not share any of the prejudiced views of Arya socialists. Instead, he was known for his secular outlook, religious tolerance, and unwavering dedication to secular values. Azad was a true advocate of the Urdu language, and his deep appreciation for its literature remained steadfast throughout his life. It is unjust to label such an individual as an Arya Samaji. Unfortunately, Azad is no longer with us, but had he been, Professor Jain would not have dared to make such an erroneous claim.

Jagannath Azad consistently expressed his disapproval of the sectarianism and divisive activities of his contemporaries. This was evident in his poignant poem about the tragic demolition of Babri Masjid on December 6, 1992, which resonated deeply with anyone who possessed a sense of pride and compassion. It is difficult to imagine that someone with such beliefs could be considered an Arya Samaji, (a follower of a reformist Hindu movement).

Under the leadership of Madan Mohan Malviya, the Hindu Samaj, a Hindu organization, was founded in Allahabad in 1880. Malviya, who later became a prominent leader of the Indian National Congress, took on the responsibility of promoting the Hindi language and the Nagari script. In 1884, the organization launched a vigorous campaign to petition for Hindi in the North-Western Provinces, the Government of Oudh, and the Government of India. That same year, a conference was held in Allahabad under the Hindu Samaj's banner, where discussions focused on establishing Hindi as an official language in courts. Delegates from across northern India attended the conference. The organization continued organizing meetings, discussions, and protests opposing Urdu and advocating for Hindi. However, in 1894, when the Hindu society began to lose momentum, Pandit Madan Mohan Malviya aligned himself with the *Nagari Pracharni Sabha* of Banaras.

Prejudiced inclinations and anti-Urdu ideologies persisted at both organizational and individual levels. Efforts were made to link Hindi with nationalism on one side and Hinduism (referred to as Hindutva) on the other. This trend was exemplified in the slogan coined by Pratab Narayan Mishra in the late 19th century: "Hindi, Hindu, Hindustan." Along with Mishra, many Hindus of that period shared biases against Urdu and went to great lengths to promote Hindi. Key figures such as Swami Dayanand Saraswati, Shri Ram Pahlori, Lala Lajpat Rai, and Pandit Madan Mohan Malviya played significant roles in this context. In addition, several other 19th-century Hindus like Ayodhya Prasad Khatri, Babu (Raja) Shiv Prasad, and Bharatendu Harishchandra vigorously sought to eliminate Urdu from courts, offices, and schools in favor of Hindi. This collective effort gave rise to the "Hindi Movement," also known as the *Khari Boli Ka Andolan.* Shakti Kanth Mishra, an alumnus of Banaras Hindu University, wrote a book titled *Khari Boli Ka Andolan,* published in 1956 by the *Nagari Pracharni Sabha,* Banaras.

Ayodhya Prasad Khatri, from Muzaffarpur (Bihar), was a strong proponent of Khari Boli Hindi poetry. In 1887, he published a book titled *Khari Boli Ka Padya,* which contained prejudiced remarks about Urdu—remarks that continue to be echoed by Hindi proponents today. Khatri regarded Braj Bhasha and Khari Boli Hindi as distinct languages but acknowledged the connection between Khari Boli and Urdu, considering them the same language with the only difference being the script. He also urged Urdu speakers to abandon the Persian script in favor of the Devanagari script. Khatri is credited with originating three prevalent anti-Urdu ideologies of the present and recent past: advocating for Urdu to adopt the style of Hindi, suggesting a change in its script, and promoting the idea that Urdu and Hindi are one language.

Thus began the movement to modify Hindi by removing Arabic and Persian words from Urdu and replacing them with Sanskrit words. This trend of making Hindi heavily

Sanskritized also gained momentum in the 19th century. Raja Lakshman Singh of Agra led this movement. He translated many Sanskrit texts into Hindi, filling the language with difficult Sanskrit terms. Christopher King notes that Singh deliberately avoided using Arabic or Persian words. In 1878, Raja Lakshman Singh published his Hindi translation of Kalidasa's Sanskrit work *Raghudas,* in the preface of which he expressed his separatist views regarding Hindi and Urdu:

"In my opinion, Hindi and Urdu are two very different languages. The Hindus of this country speak Hindi, while the Muslims and the Hindus who have studied Persian speak Urdu. Sanskrit words are widely used in Hindi, just as Arabic and Persian words are widely used in Urdu. There is no need to use Arabic and Persian words while speaking Hindi. Nor do I speak Hindi, a language rich in Arabic and Persian words." (Reference: Christopher King, *One Language, Two Scripts...,* p.31).

According to Christopher King, Raja Lakshman Singh's statement clearly indicates that, by that time and even earlier, Hindi had been recognized as the language of Hindus, while Urdu had become associated with Muslims. The sharp division between Hindi and Urdu, initiated by Lallulal Kavi on religious grounds at Fort William College, gradually gained acceptance among Hindus as they embraced Hindi as their distinct language, separate from Urdu. In addition to this, there was a concerted campaign to remove Urdu from government offices and courts, and a movement emerged advocating for the adoption of Hindi in government and educational institutions.

In the latter half of the nineteenth century, Babu Shiv Prasad of Banaras, an Inspector of Schools in the Provincial Education Department, played a crucial role in sparking the Hindi movement. While his views may have evolved over time, he remained a staunch supporter of Hindi and the Devanagari script throughout his life. He actively promoted the removal of Urdu from government offices and courts, pushing for Hindi to take its place. This biased and aggressive stance towards Urdu is evident in a memorandum he presented to the British government in 1868 titled "Court Characters in the Upper Provinces of India." This memorandum targeted both Urdu and Muslims, linking them closely, which led to its being kept for private circulation to maintain its secrecy. Even though times have changed significantly, Gyan Chand Jain's book from 2005 reflects a similar attitude toward Urdu and Muslims, comparing them to Babu Raja Shiv Prasad. Professor Jain stated that "most

Hindu writers of Urdu have a Shiv Prasad in their hearts"
(*One Language ... p.278*). Despite 137 years passing, it
seems little has changed in the sentiments expressed by
figures like Shiv Prasad and Professor Jain.

In his memorandum, Babu Shiv Prasad harshly criticized
the government for implementing a linguistic policy that, in
his view, imposed Urdu, a foreign language written in the
Persian script, upon the people. He argued that "reading
Persian means to become a Persian," implying that learning
the language corrupted one's identity and rendered their
nationality void.

Shiv Prasad ultimately appealed to the government to
remove the Persian script from courts, just as it had
abolished the Persian language, and to enforce Hindi instead.
He believed that this step would bring many benefits, chief
among them the restoration of Hindu nationality (*One
Language, Two Scripts*, p.31).

In his book, Professor Jain refers to Shiv Prasad's 1868
memorandum but refrains from criticizing Shiv Prasad's
biased views, anti-Muslim sentiments, or his statements.
Instead, Professor Jain endorses Shiv Prasad's position as
being entirely justified. Professor Jain writes:

"The efforts made by Hindus to rectify the suppression of Hindu civilization during the 700-year Muslim rule and its degradation to a lower status after the 1857 uprising, what is wrong with that?" (*One Language, Two Scripts*, p.176).

When Sir Syed Ahmad Khan naturally responded to this malicious memorandum, it is unlikely his reaction would have been as hostile as Professor Jain claims. Professor Jain writes:

"When Hindus expressed their desire to embrace Hindi instead of Urdu, Sir Syed Sahib was deeply dismayed, and for the rest of his life, he made it his policy to uproot the Hindus. Sir Syed's only demand from the Hindus was for them to acknowledge the presence of an Islamic government in India" (*One Language, Two Scripts*, p.18).

It is ironic that Professor Jain interprets Sir Syed Ahmad Khan's efforts to express regret over the forced removal of Urdu from courts, offices, and educational institutions, as well as his advocacy for unity, harmony, and brotherhood among communities, as "uprooting Hindus." This portrayal is a clear example of negative thinking and a misrepresentation of Sir Syed's intentions.

Among Shiv Prasad's contemporaries, Bhartendu Harish Chandra holds significant importance. He, too, hailed from Banaras. Despite his young age and a short life span of only 35 years, he established himself as one of the most prominent early writers in modern Hindi literature. Bhartendu Harish Chandra is widely recognized as the first consistent author of Khari Boli Hindi. According to Professor Jain, it is essential to acknowledge that Bhartendu was not against Urdu (*One Language, Two Scripts, p.177*). However, Christopher King notes that Bhartendu was even more fervent in supporting and advocating for both Hindi and the Devanagari script than Babu Shiv Prasad. King observes,

"Bhartendu championed the cause of both Hindi and the Nagari script even more vigorously than Prasad" (King, *One Language, Two Scripts,* p.32).

Furthermore, Shakti Kanth Mishra writes that:

Bhartendu initiated a movement to promote and publish Hindi upon his arrival in the Hindi-speaking region, which eventually developed into a collective revolution spanning the entire Hindi belt (Khari Boli Movement, p.96).

Bhartendu was a proponent of Khari Boli prose but had reservations about its suitability for poetry. He considered Braj Bhasha more appropriate for poetic expression and composed poetry in that language himself. Although he was also an Urdu poet, using the poetic name "Rasa," his intentions towards Urdu were not supportive. In his writings, he often ridiculed Urdu and presented it in a derogatory manner. Not only did he criticize Urdu itself, but he also targeted its supporters, humiliating and cursing them. This disdainful attitude is best exemplified in his work 'Siyapa,' published in his journal 'Harish Chandri Chandrika' in 1874. Professor Jain did not give sufficient attention to Bhartendu's stance in this regard (*One Language, Two Scripts,* p.177).

Bhartendu's literary works cover a wide range of themes. One of his books is '*Agarwalun ki Utpatti*' (*The Origin of Agarwals*). In its preface, he writes:

"Agarwals are from the southwestern region, and their language, spoken by both men and women, is Khari Boli, which is equivalent to Urdu" (Rahi; *Khari Boli: Sauroop and Sayiteek Parampara*, p.25).

Professor Jain has provided incorrect information regarding the language of Agarwal entrepreneurs, stating that their language is "Khara Boli" but never mentioning Urdu. Additionally, he claims that no section of Hindus, especially women, practiced Urdu. In his book, Professor Jain writes:

"I want to clarify that Bhartendu referred to the language of Agarwals as 'Khari Boli' and not Urdu. Among Hindus, Kashmiri Pandits and Kayasths used to practice Urdu, while only Punjabi Khatris among Khatris practiced it. There is no specific reason behind the uncommon practice of Urdu among Agarwals. Regarding women, no section of Hindus practiced Urdu" (p.179).

Regarding the points Professor Jain made about Bhartendu, he did not provide any references to support his claims. He did not consult Bhartendu's '*Agarwalu ki Utpatti*' or Omkar Rahi's '*Khari Boli: Sauroop aur Sahiteek Parampara*' (1975). Instead, he made assumptions, which may have been advantageous for him but prevented him from stating the truth. Therefore, it is unclear why he emphasizes the loyalty of intellectuals to truthfulness (p.31).

In his book '*Agarwalu ki Utpatti*,' Bhartendu clearly states that Agarwals belong to the southwestern region and that

131

their language, both for men and women, is Khari Boli, which is synonymous with Urdu. This fact is also cited by Omarkar Rahi in his book on page 25.

Professor Jain has distorted Bhartendu's statement and presented it without any proper reference. He has spread false information, which is something he should be ashamed of.

From this excerpt of Bhartendu's book, we can conclude the following:

1. Agarwals were inhabitants of the southwestern regions and spoke Urdu.
2. Not only the men but also the women of Agarwals practiced Urdu.
3. During that period, Khari Boli was another term used for Urdu.

Professor Jain should be well aware that the fundamental principle of research is to gather information from original sources before forming narratives and opinions. However, Professor Jain failed to analyze Bhartendu's actual quote and instead interpreted it according to personal preferences and biases. Such research practices are not only unethical but also deceptive.

As evident from Bhartendu's statement, Urdu was not only the language of Agarwals but also of their women. Furthermore, Bhartendu's statement confirms that Khari Boli was another term used for Urdu. It is worth mentioning that some Hindus in the 19th century, such as Ayodhya Prasad Khatri, referred to Khari Boli as Urdu. Other Hindus who supported Hindi poetry in Braj Bhasha also used the term Khari Boli for Urdu and opposed poetry written in Khari Boli, as they believed it would be considered Urdu. Bhartendu shared a similar perspective and encouraged the use of Braj Bhasha for Hindi poetry, not preferring poetry in Khari Boli Hindi. Although he would recite verses in Urdu using "Rasa" as his poetic name.

Towards the end of the 19th century, during a period marked by significant unrest in the Hindi Movement, which unfortunately manifested as aggressive communal riots, the *Nagari Parchaarni Sabha* was established in Banaras in 1893. This assembly dedicated its efforts to promoting, publicizing, and strengthening the Hindi language and Nagari script. The *Sabha* received support from influential figures of the time, including prominent personalities such as Pt. Madan Mohan Malviya and Sir G.A. Grierson.

Its primary objective was to introduce Hindi and the Nagari script in government offices and courts. In 1895, during the visit of the Lieutenant Governor of Awadh, Sir Antony Macdonald, to Banaras, a delegation led by Maharaja Pratab Narayan Singh of Ajodhiya, accompanied by prominent figures like Pandit Madan Mohan Malviya, Sir Sundar Lal, Raja Mada, and Raja Awadh, presented him with a commendatory address. In response, Sir Macdonald expressed his keen interest in their appeal and acknowledged their plea to implement the Devanagari script instead of Urdu in official capacities. Although he stated that an immediate decision could not be made, he assured the delegation that their concerns would be considered in the near future. (Ref: Sham Sundar Das 'My Own Story' p. 30, as cited by Hukum Chand Nair, *Urdu ke Masail*, p. 130)

On March 2, 1898, when Sir Macdonald visited Allahabad, the delegates met him again and presented a memorandum containing 60,000 signatures, urging the adoption of Hindi as the official language and for educational purposes. Hukum Chand Nair explains that this memorandum was an abstract of Pandit Madan Mohan Malviya's book titled *Court Character and Primary Education in the North-West Provinces and Oudh.* In this book, Malviya highlighted the limitations of the Urdu script and advocated for the adoption of Hindi and the Nagari script, aligning with the objectives of the *Nagari Pracharni Sabha.* Nair further emphasizes that Malviya's book played a significant role in shaping Sir Macdonald's decision on April 18, 1900. (Ibid)

Sir Antony Macdonald held a strong bias against Urdu and actively supported Hindi and the Nagari script. Before his appointment as Lieutenant Governor of the North-West Provinces and Oudh, he had held important positions in Bihar and Bengal, where he played a crucial role in implementing Hindi in government offices. The proponents of the Hindi Movement were elated when Macdonald assumed the position of Governor General, as they had high hopes for his support. As expected, on April 18, 1900, Macdonald issued an order granting Hindi and the Nagari script equal status to Urdu in courts and government offices. This decision was a significant achievement for the pioneers of the Hindi Movement, especially the members of the *Nagari Pracharni Sabha.* However, Macdonald's decision caused unrest in Urdu-speaking regions, particularly among the Muslim community. Protests emerged in various locations, with Muslim organizations and notable individuals expressing their discontent with the decision.

On May 13, 1900, Nawab Mohsin-ul-Mulk, the Honorary Secretary of MAO College in Aligarh, delivered a powerful speech during a protest led by Nawab Lateef Ali Khan, raising awareness about the disadvantages of the government's decision. It was decided during this protest to present a memorandum to the government, and a detailed record of the protest was submitted. Macdonald, however, viewed the protest with disappointment, considering it an attack on his government's policies. When Mohsin-ul-Mulk attempted to engage in dialogue with Macdonald to clarify any misunderstandings, Macdonald refused, stating:

"If it is possible to discuss the Urdu-Nagari issue through writing, then your visit to Nainital is unnecessary" (Ref: Mohd Amin Zubairi, *Hayaat Mohsin,* pp. 88-89).

Similarly, on August 18, 1900, large-scale protests erupted in Lucknow under the leadership of Mohsin-ul-Mulk. This protest was organized by the Central Urdu Defense Association, established specifically for this purpose, with Nawab Mohsin-ul-Mulk serving as its president. Macdonald became aware of these events. During his visit to Aligarh (as the patron of MAO College), he expressed his displeasure to the college trustees, blaming the Urdu Defense Association for the unrest and accusing students, faculty, trustees, and Mohsin-ul-Mulk of participating in the protests. Macdonald even warned that if such activities continued, the government would withdraw its funding (ibid, p.160). As a result, Nawab Mohsin-ul-Mulk resigned as the president of the Central Urdu Defense Association and distanced himself from future movements. Eventually, the Urdu Defense Association dissolved, primarily due to Macdonald's actions.

As previously mentioned, there was a significant rise in the Hindi movement in the second half of the 19th century, reaching its peak by the century's end. For his own purposes, the movement linked Hindi with "Hindutva" and "Hindi Nationalism." The idea that "Hindi" and "Hindu" were equivalent spread widely. In contrast to Urdu, Hindi was promoted as the "Hindu identity," fostering hatred for both Urdu and Muslims. According to Christopher King, after India's partition, this movement contributed to the federalism that arose in the region. King elaborates on the Hindi Movement's focus:

"The essence of the movement lay in efforts to *differentiate* Hindi from Urdu and to make Hindi a symbol of Hindu culture. Seen in this light, the Hindi movement formed part of a much broader process of the heightening of communal awareness in pre-independence India, a transformation of ethnic groups into communities and nationalities which culminated in the birth of Pakistan in 1947." (*One Langauge, Two Scripts,* pp. 10-11)

King further illustrates the divisive nature of the Hindi Movement:

"We can look at the whole history of the Hindi movement as a deliberate attempt to increase differentiation (to make Hindi more and more different from Urdu and to reduce assimilation (to discourage Hindus from any attachment to Urdu), while the countervailing Urdu movement strove to accomplish the opposite". (*One Language, Two Scripts*, p. 176).

The primary goal of the Hindi movement was to disrupt the centuries-old linguistic unity and collaboration between

Hindus and Muslims in northern India, a bond deeply rooted in the shared use of Urdu. Recognizing that Hindi's progress and advancement would be difficult without undermining this linguistic harmony, supporters of the Hindi movement sought to dismantle it. They propagated the idea that Urdu belonged solely to Muslims and that Hindi was synonymous with Hindu identity. As a result, they attempted to establish a general belief that being a Hindu meant supporting Hindi, while supporting Urdu meant aligning with Islam. Some Hindus even went so far as to believe that it was impossible to be a devout Hindu and still advocate for Urdu. Christopher King addresses this issue, noting:

> "The other side of the divide came with the beginning of the Hindi movement in the 1860s when some Hindus began to assert that one could no longer be a good Hindu and an advocate of Urdu at the same time. This movement made deliberate changes in Khari Boli which eventually resulted in a highly Sanskritized Hindi. The split in the common trunk of Hindi and Urdu, Khari Boli, which began with the growth of one major branch, Persianized Urdu, now continued with the growth of another major branch, Sanskritized Hindi. The process of multi-symbol

congruence now commenced in earnest and culminated in slogans such as 'Hindi, Hindu, Hindustan' whose creators saw no room for non-Hindi speakers and non-Hindus in Hindustan. We might go so far as to call this process the 'Sanskritization of Urdu' or at least the 'Sanskritization of Khari Boli'."

(*One Language, Two Scripts*, p. 177).

In the 19th century, several anti-Urdu organizations emerged in North India, aiming to eliminate Urdu from courts, offices, and educational institutions. However, Professor Jain's book overlooks these movements, choosing instead to place blame on Muslims for obstructing the growth of Hindi. The decision by Hindus to adopt Hindi over Urdu is a separate issue that cannot solely be attributed to Muslim actions.

When Sir Syed Ahmad Khan showed his natural reaction on Baba Shiv Peasad's highly divisive and inflammatory memorandum of 1868 and the malevolent statements made against Urdu in that memorandum, Jain sahib said: When the Hindus wanted to adopt Hindi instead of Urdu, Syed Sahib became angry (see *Ek Bhasha...* p. 18). It is a separate topic of discussion why the Hindus desired to adopt Hindi over

Urdu. Was it because they were Hindus? Did all Hindus want to adopt Hindi instead of Urdu? It is evident that a large section of Hindus had a sound understanding and professional knowledge of Urdu. They did not face any difficulty or awkwardness in working with Urdu in courts and offices. The three sects of Hindus—Kayasths, Khatris, and Kashmiri Brahmins—had deep connections with Urdu, considering it their own language. Due to their knowledge of Urdu, they had no issues securing jobs in courts and government offices where Urdu was the official language. Not only did these people read and write Urdu, but they also had no excuse for not learning Persian. While other Hindu sects also studied Urdu and Persian, these three sects had notable representation among Urdu speakers. They also held a dominant presence in government jobs. Despite the common cultural and linguistic traditions shared between these three Hindu sects (Kayasths, Kashmiri Brahmins, and Khatris) and Muslims, this commonality did not affect the religious identity of these Hindu groups. When Sir Syed Ahmed Khan responded to Babu Shiv Prasad's memorandum, he recognized the longstanding linguistic and cultural connection that had united Hindus and Muslims for centuries. He feared that any language conflict could result in the division of these communities. Sir Syed stressed the importance of preserving this bond, despite the political agendas of Western leaders and the nationalist movement. In a letter to Mohsin ul Mulk from London on April 29, 1870, Sir Syed voiced his concern that the memorandum would provoke Hindus to abolish Urdu and its Perso-Arabic script, which symbolized the identity of Muslims. He saw this as a tactic to further widen the rift between Hindus and Muslims and to prevent any chance of unity. He wrote:

"I have received another piece of news that deeply saddens and worries me. It concerns the movement of Babu Prasad and the general sentiment among the Hindu people that the Urdu language, along with the influence of Persian, which they associate with Muslims, should be eradicated... This is a plan that will lead to disagreement between Hindus and Muslims." (—) (*Sarras Masood* (compiled), *Letters of Sir Syed Ahmad*, p. 88; with references from Soraya Hussain, *Sir Syed Ahmad Khan and His Reign*, p. 255).

This reaction of Sir Syed Ahmad Khan was not due to any linguistic prejudice, but was based on good intentions and in the national interest. However, Gian Chand Jain was not pleased with this reaction. Why? Did he not appreciate the linguistic sharing, unity, and national cohesion between the two major communities of India, i.e., Hindus and Muslims?.

Sir Syed referred to Urdu as the symbol of Muslims, and Prof. Jain objected to this as well. But why did Jain Sahib not object to Hindu figures like Lalluji Lal or Suneeti Kumar Chatterjee, who referred to Urdu as "Yamini Basha," "Maleesh Basha," or "Musalmaani Basha"—terms implying that Urdu was the language of Muslims? If Professor Jain had a deeper understanding of the social, cultural, and linguistic history of Hindi, he would recognize that it was Hindus themselves who labeled Urdu as the "Musalmaani Basha" or "language of Muslims." The entire Hindi movement was predicated on the belief that Urdu was the language of Muslims (Urdu = Muslims), while Hindi represented Hindus (Hindi = Hindus). In contrast, Urdu proponents believed that Urdu was a shared language for both communities (Urdu = Hindus + Muslims). Why did Professor Jain take offense when Sir Syed Ahmed Khan expressed the same viewpoint that Hindu leaders and proponents of the Hindi movement had repeatedly voiced? Shouldn't it have caused the same discomfort? Sir Syed would not have identified Urdu as the identity of Muslims had Babu Shiv Prasad not submitted such a divisive and anti-Urdu memorandum. In reality, the blame lies with Babu Shiv Prasad, not with Sir Syed Ahmed Khan, as Sir Syed never anticipated that Hindus would be driven apart due to language issues.

The focus remained on the Hindi and Nagari movements, as well as anti-Urdu activities, because Urdu was continuously under attack during that period. It was frequently labeled as a foreign language or a Muslim language, reinforcing the belief that "Urdu = Muslims." This narrative was used to alienate Hindus from Urdu. Some narrow-minded Hindus even went so far as to call it "Maleesh Basha" or the language of prostitutes. In the literary works of the Hindi movement, there were frequent instances of mockery, jokes, and derogatory references to the Urdu language. Other Hindu organizations, initially formed for religious reform and welfare, became deeply involved in promoting Hindi and the Nagari script. Following the establishment of the *Nagari Pracharni Sabha* in Banaras (1893), anti-Urdu activities escalated, and the Hindi movement reached its peak. This culminated in the decision made by Sir Antonni Macdonald, the Lieutenant Governor of the North-Western Provinces and Oudh, on April 18, 1900. This decision sparked a new linguistic conflict in North India, leaving the Muslim community worried and agitated. This linguistic conflict had profound social, political, and cultural consequences, marking a significant turning point in the history of Urdu—a tragedy that left an indelible mark on the language and its speakers.

Chapter One: One Language: Two Scripts, Two Literatures

1 In this context, Shamsur Rahman Farooqi's article *"One Language, Two Scripts, Two Literatures"* published in the April 2006 issue of *Kitabnama* (New Delhi), holds significant importance. During this period, thought-provoking articles and critiques by Shamim Hanafi, poets Ashiq Harganvi, Athar Farooqi, and Mohammad Arif Iqbal were published regarding Gyan Chand Jain's controversial book *Fiya*. Additionally, articles by Naeem Kaur (*Sadaye Urdu*) and Asad Sanai (*Al-Ansar*) were released. However, the editorial styles of Sajid Rashid (*New Paper*) and Krishna Kumar (*Lush*) were somewhat different.

2 In his article *Urdu-Hindi or Indian Inclusive Linguistic Study* (Third Edition, Development Urdu Bureau, New Delhi, 1992), Gyan Chand Jain writes, "I register my mother tongue as Urdu in the census, although my parents and grandparents did not know Urdu. They had some familiarity with Hindi. No one dares to say that their language is different from that of their parents or spouse, but in the census, my

language is listed as Urdu, while my wife's is listed as Hindi." (p. 160).

3   Gyan Chand Jain received formal training in linguistics at Deccan College, Pune, and authored numerous essays on linguistic topics in his books *Linguistic Studies* (1973) and *General Linguistics* (1985).

Chapter Two: Communal Thinking and Negative Perception

1. *A House Divided: The Origin and Development of Hindi/Hindavi* by Amrit Roy was published in 1984 by Oxford University Press, Delhi. Rakim Al-Haruf wrote an article on this book in Urdu, which was published on May 1, 1987, in *Hamari Zaban* (New Delhi). This article, titled "Amrit Roy and the Problem of Hindi-Urdu," is included in Rakim Al-Haruf's book *Linguistic Perspectives* (New Delhi: Bahiri Publications, 1997).

2. In one of his essays, Gyan Chand Jain writes about the origin of Urdu: "In my opinion, the origin of Urdu is nothing but the emergence of a standing dialect." He further elaborates, "The birth of Urdu

was the birth of the standing dialect, which arose from the *Apbhransh* in the eleventh and twelfth centuries and was spoken in regions like Jodhpur, Meerut, and Moradabad, among others." (See *Linguistic Studies*, 3rd ed., New Delhi: Progress Urdu Bureau, 1992, pp. 82 and 95).

Chapter Three: Urdu Language, Urdu-Speaking Muslims, and Urdu Literature

1. The title of the poem by Jagannath Azad is "Babri Masjid." It was written on December 6, 1992, the same day the Babri Masjid was demolished. Upon hearing the news, Azad writes that he was overwhelmed with grief, which inspired him to write this poem. It is included in Azad's poetry collection *Naseem Hijaz* (New Delhi: Mhumrid Memorial Literary Society, 1999).

2. Jahangir married a Rajput princess, Maan Mati (or Jagat Gosain), from whom Prince Khurram (later known as Shah Jahan) was born.

Chapter Four: Khari Boli Hindi

1. Gyan Chand Jain earlier recognized this fact, but his views changed significantly when writing *Ek Bhasha*. In one of his essays written around 35 years ago, "The Linguistic Relationship of Urdu and Hindi" (included in *Linguistic Studies*, First Edition, 1973), Jain notes, "The composition of Hindi prose at Fort William College included Arabic-Persian words." (p. 185).

2. In his book *Ek Bhasha*, Gyan Chand Jain overlooks certain statements by Chandradhar Sharma Guleri and Jagannath Das. These statements assert that Urdu serves as the basis for Hindi.

3. In addition to Grierson and Kay, a contemporary scholar, Christopher R. King, in his book *One Language, Two Scripts*, writes on page 27: "Lallu Lal, while writing *Prem Sagar*, deliberately omitted words from languages associated with Muslims."

Chapter Five: Urdu's Precedence over Hindi

1. The history of the Muslim conquest of Delhi dates back to 1193. From this period onward, a systematic process of linguistic mixing began in Delhi and its surrounding areas.

2. Gyan Chand Jain, in his book *Ancient Books of Spoken Hindi up to 1800* (pp. 300 to 302), includes some books that belong to Braj Bhasha and some unauthenticated works, such as Gang Koi's prose. The *Chand Chhand Brannan* campaign has been proven to be fraudulent, but certain scholars have authenticated it. However, Jain Sahib considers it legitimate.

3. The story *Mehr -Afroz-o-Dilbar* by Isvi Khan Bahadur is recognized as the first prose story in Urdu from North India, composed between 1732 and 1759. The only known copy, owned by Agha Haider Hasan, was first compiled by Masood Hussain Khan in 1966. It was published in Hyderabad.

4. More details can be found in Chapter Seven.

Chapter Six: Hindi Imperialism and Urdu Language

1. See B.G. Mishra's essay "Language Movements in the Hindi Region" (*Anna Malai*, 1979, note).

2. The 1991 Census of India records a total of 114 languages. Out of these, 18 languages—1) Hindi, 2) Bengali, 3) Telugu, 4) Marathi, 5) Tamil, 6) Urdu, 7) Gujarati, 8) Kannada, 9) Malayalam, 10) Oriya, 11)

Punjabi, 12) Assamese, 13) Sindhi, 14) Nepali, 15) Konkani, 16) Manipuri, 17) Kashmiri, and 18) Sanskrit—are categorized as Scheduled Languages because they are mentioned in the Eighth Schedule of the Constitution of India. The remaining 96 languages are categorized as non-scheduled languages. However, these non-scheduled languages are also spoken as "Mother Tongues" in India. The number of languages spoken in India exceeds this count. According to the 1991 Census, the total number of mother tongues recorded is 216, each with at least 100,000 (one hundred thousand) speakers. For the purpose of the census, these 216 mother tongues were grouped into 14 linguistic categories based on morphological similarities. These 14 linguistic categories encompass the 114 scheduled and non-scheduled languages of India. Among these linguistic categories, "Hindi" is the largest in terms of the number of speakers. This category includes 28 mother tongues, including Hindi itself. The total number of Hindi speakers as a mother tongue is recorded as 528,432,233 (five hundred twenty-eight million, four hundred thirty-two thousand, two hundred thirty-three). The total number of speakers of the remaining 47 mother tongues, as well as some other "other" mother tongues, is 829,103,839 (eighty-two million, nine hundred three thousand, eight hundred thirty-nine). The names of other mother tongues are not listed because each has fewer than 100,000 (one hundred thousand) speakers. The category of mother tongues is named after the mother tongue with the largest number of speakers within it. For example, among the 48 mother tongues spoken in North and Central India, Hindi has the largest number of speakers, and hence, the category is named "Hindi." Within this category, the remaining 47 mother tongues are often referred to as dialects. However, it should be noted that the term "dialects" is not officially used in the Census of India. Hindi itself is considered a fully-fledged language and is recognized as such, unlike the other 47 mother tongues grouped under it, which are often considered smaller in scale. . (See -1 Census of India (1991, Series-1: Languages, India and States by M. Vijayanunni See Christopher R. Gang, *One Language, Two Scripts* (177).

3. See Christopher R. King's *One Language, Two Scripts* (p. 177).

4. See Santi Kumar Chatterji's *Indo-Aryan and Hindi* (p. 209).

5. Gyan Chand Jain writes in his essay "Linguistic Relationship of Urdu and Hindi": "The true situation is that Urdu and Hindi are two forms of the same dialect. Urdu's written form was shaped by Hindi traditions and the Nagari script, but its present form is an embellished and refined version. The literary and linguistic capital of these two forms has diverged so much that denying this reality is ignoring the facts." (See *Linguistic Studies*, First Edition, p. 204).

6. Some Hindi speakers deny Urdu's existence as a separate language. For example, prominent Hindi writers and politicians like Sampoorna Nand did not recognize Urdu speakers as a linguistic minority, as doing so would mean recognizing Urdu as an independent language. He regarded Urdu as merely a style of Hindi. At the 68th anniversary of the *Nagari Sabha* in Benares (1961), he stated that Urdu speakers should not be considered a linguistic minority. (See All Ahmad Sarwar's *Sampoornanand Ji and Urdu Content Urdu Tehreek*, p. 218).

Chapter Seven: The Outcome of *Prem Sagar*

1. The Christian calendar (AD) is 57 years behind Sambat. Subtracting 57 years from Sambat gives the corresponding year in AD.

2. These books were first written in Urdu and later transcribed into the Nagari script.

3. Prominent Hindi writer and intellectual Ramchandra Shukla notes that "had Lallu Lal not known Urdu, he would not have been able to remove Arabic-Persian words from *Prem Sagar*". (See *History of Hindi Sahitya*, p. 365).

4. In his book *Human Studies* (1973), Gyan Chand Jain acknowledges that" Arabic-Persian words were removed from Hindi prose in Fort William College and replaced by Sanskrit *Tatsama* words. "(p. 185).

Chapter Eight: Urdu, Hindi, Hindustani and The Fort William College

1. Some researchers believe that Gujari has no connection with Gujarat. For example, Suniti Kumar Chatterjee asserts that "this Gujari dialect is not Gujarati at all." However, Burhanuddin Janam, a

Deccani (Bijapuri) poet, refers to the language as "Gujari" (See Suniti Kumar Chatterjee, *Indo-Aryan and Hindi*, p. 206).

2. The term *Malechh Bhasha*, used in a derogatory sense, is attributed to Chandradhar Sharma Guleri. Shattikanth Mishra writes in his book *Khadi Boli Ka Andolan*: "Guleriji believed that the standing dialect was entirely linked to the Muslims and referred to it as *Malechh Bhasha* (Khadi Boli Ka Andolan, p. 9).

3. In his book *The Oriental Linguist*, Gilchrist refers to Hindustani (Urdu) as "the popular dialect of India."

4. After Lallu Lal's *Prem Sagar* (1803) and Sidal Mishra's *Naskh Pakhyan* (1803), no significant works in spoken Hindi were produced until the mid-19th century. Eminent Hindi scholar Ramchandra Shukla admits that the period between 1803 and 1858 is a complete void in terms of prose writing. (See Gyan Chand Jain's *Linguistic Studies*, p. 177).

5. See Shattikanth Mishra's *Khadi Boli Ka Andolan*, p. 62.

6. Examples from Gilchrist's *A Dictionary, English and Hindustani* were referenced on page 62 of Muhammad Ateeq Siddiqui's book *Gilchrist and His Testament*.

7. See Shattikanth Mishra's *Khadi Boli Ka Andolan*, p. 69.

Chapter Nine: Anti-Urdu Movements and Tendencies

1. Jagannath Azad's poem titled "Babri Masjid" is included in his poetry collection *Naseem Hijaz* (New Delhi: Mhumrun Memorial Literary Society, 1999).

2. Ram Vilas Sharma, in his book *Bharat Ki Bhasha Samsya* (p. 311), quotes two poems by Bharatendu Harishchandra.

3. However, Christopher R. King, in his book *One Language Two Scripts*, provides detailed accounts of the activities of the Charni *Sabha* (Benares) related to the Hindi movement and the Nagari script.

4. Hukm Chand Neez discusses the incident in his article "The Greatest Tragedy of Urdu: The Decision of 18th April 1900". This article is included in his book ' Issues of Urdu: In the Light of Social and Political Movement of India'(1977).

About the Translators of This Book:

Dr. Mohmad Ashraf Bhat is a distinguished linguist with a PhD from IIT Kanpur and a postdoc from IIT Delhi. His acclaimed book "The Changing Language Roles and Linguistic Identities of the Kashmiri Speech Community", published by Cambridge Scholars UK is globally recognized. Presently, he serves as a faculty member, Department of Foreign Languages, Faculty of Arts and Humanities, Jazan University, Jazan KSA.

Dr. Mehnaz Rashid pursued her PhD in Linguistics from University of Kashmir, India. She has been associated with teaching at different colleges in Kashmir. Presently she is teaching at the Government College for Women (GCW), M.A Road, Srinagar, Kashmir, India.

Linguists Collective and Cambridge ITC Book Publishing

Website: https://bookpublishing.linguistscollective.info

Email: bp@linguistscollective.info

Interpreting & Translation Linguists Collective Agency

LC UK: +44 (0)333 240 0139

LC Ireland and Europe: +353 (0)96 96404

Rest of the World (WhatsApp, WeChat, Signal):

+44 (0)730 737 7430

Linguists Collective Ltd

38 Mill Street

Bedford

MK40 3HD

United Kingdom